T0162669

Learning *How to Fly*

RUTH L. MIDSUMMER

Order this book online at www.trafford.com
or email orders@trafford.com

Most Trafford titles are also available at major online book retailers.

Printed in the United States of America.

ISBN: 978-1-4907-4757-6 (sc)
ISBN: 978-1-4907-4758-3 (hc)
ISBN: 978-1-4907-4759-0 (e)

Library of Congress Control Number: 2014917237

Trafford rev. 09/25/2014

 www.trafford.com

North America & international
toll-free: 1 888 232 4444 (USA & Canada)
fax: 812 355 4082

■ CHAPTER 1

I followed the attendant into the small room in the insane asylum in Taunton, Massachusetts, and took the heavy chair she offered me. The place brought back horrible memories, memories I thought I had buried deep within my mind, thought I had forgotten. They came again to haunt me as I sat and faced my sister.

Marla's empty voice spoke through twisted lips: "I had a lot of nightmares last night. I dreamed that Ma was a big lion, and I was a little kitten. There were people all around me, surrounding me. They kept repeating the same words. 'As long as you stay with me, you'll be safe. As long as you stay with Ma, you'll be safe.'"

I smothered a lump in my throat by swallowing hard. The wire mesh on the window on top of the only door reminded me of a prison. It was a cell—no pictures, no lamps, bare walls. A plain gray table separated us.

The pungent smell of disinfectant penetrated my nostrils, causing my eyes to water, but it was Marla's eyes that made me wince. She wore the dilated look of a tortured soul, that look I knew so well but never could get used to.

Why? I asked myself. Why did this have to happen? I wanted to know, needed to know. I searched my mind for reasons. A clue. Anything.

She had always wanted a child, but she had become that child. Was it her fears that had stood in her way? I used to blame her for the times when she would lay in bed for hours on end, for the times when she would overdose on drugs, although it wasn't the drugs alone that had made her ill. I used to blame her for making Mother her slave. Now I'm not so sure. Now, although I will always love her, I let God judge her.

I fought to keep back the tears; sometimes I tried not to believe it. She was a stranger to me now, someone I was seeing for the first time. Although she was two years younger than my fifty years, Marla looked ancient. It wasn't the wrinkles alone that made her look so old. Her thin lips revealed yellow teeth with big gaping holes, and years of taking medication had thinned her hair and turned it gray before its time.

There were craters in her face where blackheads had taken over, and a protruded belly was framed by limp arms—the same arms that had battered my mother more than once, smashed chairs, and shattered dishes.

I blinked back fresh tears when I remembered she was once pretty. I could still picture the blonde ponytail and innocent expression in blue eyes. I remembered too the many nights when I had prayed for my baby sister and the pain I felt when I realized slowly, through the years, that she would never recover.

As I listened to her, I was acutely aware of an old proverb that repeated in my mind: "There but for the grace of God—."

. . .

She was baptized Marla Olga Stephanie Midsummer, the youngest of four children born to Leslie and Jack Midsummer, our mother and father. Theirs was a wild courtship. He was only five feet six, but powerful, handsome and clean-cut, with reddish hair and a hint of freckles that displayed his Swedish inheritance.

"Wow" was all he could say when a friend introduced them, completely lost to the magic of love.

She smiled shyly, unaware at fifteen of the curves on her body or the heads that turned to stare.

He was four years older, had never used profanity, drank, nor used tobacco, but he loved the excitement of living on the edge. He took chances when he operated his bulldozer at work, coming a little bit closer than others to falling off the precipice, and people admired him for it. He was good.

And he was daring on his motorcycle. One day, as he was driving at high speed, he slid off a winding road on a sharp curve. He was lucky to survive the crash, which left him with a broken collar bone as well as a broken leg. Still, even though he was in formidable pain, that didn't stop his ardor. He limped for seven miles each day on crutches to see her.

When his fractures finally healed, he let her drive his "bike" on ladies' day at the cycle club. Dressed in black jodhpurs, her dark brown hair blowing in the breeze, she saw nothing but happiness in her future.

Work wasn't always easy to come by in Rhode Island in 1934, and Jack was happy when his job took them to Athol, Massachusetts during the first year of their marriage. There, the times they spent together were filled with joy, even though he had to trudge through miles of heavy snow to get to work. Her body began to swell with pregnancy.

When the job was over, they moved back to Rhode Island because the economy there was improving. And when her labor pains began during a New England nor'easter, he was aghast because they had to walk two blocks to the delivery room in Memorial Hospital in Pawtucket.

But she laughed and chided him innocently, "Why are you afraid? They're only going to cut a hole in my belly and take out the baby." No one had told her of birth and the pain.

She was knee-deep in snow, and dragged her belly over the top. The wind was fierce, and it caught the huge wide-brimmed hat she wore twice and tossed it into a snowbank. She thought it was all in fun when he had to chase it. A snowplow came by, and he tried to convince the driver to give them a lift. But he refused.

"No baby is going to be born on my plow. Besides, it's against the law."

. . .

The labor was long and hard, and she was swollen with toxic poisoning. He paced in front of the delivery room for twelve hours and smoked three packs of cigarettes. But she was young and strong, and their first child, a boy, was born on January 23, 1935. They named him Samuel after his brother who had been killed in a motorcycle accident and her brother who was hit by a train and died shortly afterward. They vowed this Samuel would have a full life. They would see to it.

"He's all boy," he beamed to his wife in the hospital. "You've made me so happy."

. . .

In spite of the love and the caring, troubles began to smolder like a sore that festered. He was under a lot of pressure at work. They demanded more of him—more chances, more stress on his already jagged nerves.

She was used to getting her own way. She was delicate like a gazelle, and he was young with lots of hormones, as is natural. The bedroom became an arena.

"Not again. It hurts," she would scream at his demands.

She avoided sex like an evil woe, which did not help to bolster his male ego. To ease the pressure, he began to stop in at the local bar nights after work with the guys.

She became pregnant again. More pressure. He got so angry one night he became violent and kicked her in the stomach when she turned away from him in the bedroom. She was crushed. Now he had threatened the baby, and for the first time she began to consider breaking off the marriage.

Even so, our family continued to grow. They had three more children. I was number two. My younger brother Jack came eleven months after me. We called him Junior. Marla Olga Stephanie was last.

Every Christmas, my father used to drag home a tree and decorate it with lights and balls and all sorts of pretty things. Then on the night before Christmas, he always told us to look out the window for Santa Claus, and he would pick out a tiny star I confess I could never see and tell us it was Santa.

"See those lights in the sky? He's coming! Quick, get into bed. If he catches you up, you won't get any toys."

Then we'd run for our bedroom and try to sleep. The next morning, the toys would be piled up to the ceiling.

But I hated to get close to him because his breath stunk like whiskey. One day he came home with no pay. I think my mother was mad because he slept on the floor that night. When he awoke, he rocked his head from side to side. He cried like a wounded puppy. Then he picked up his whiskey bottle which was beside him and shook it. It was empty.

"Crap!" he yelled as he threw it into the kitchen sink. A big chunk of the sink flew out. It was our brand new sink. It had been so white and so pretty. But it was ruined. Then Dad looked at the hole in the wall that he had punched with his fist the day before. He hid his face in his hands and cried.

But I felt that he crossed us when he told people his kids had done it.

I loved Dad, but he was hurting Mom. Sometimes he put his hands around her throat and choked her. And what was he doing behind the bedroom door?

One day, when he told her to "get in that bedroom" and forced her to go inside, I said in a voice as gruff as I could make it, "All right, you old Jack Midsummer."

He sounded like thunder when he came out of the room. "Who said that?"

I was already under my bed hiding. I was frightened, but no one told on me.

And I'll never forget the first day of kindergarten. Mom had dressed me up in a pretty dress and put my hair in pigtails.

I looked ugly, and I felt everyone was staring at me, so I started to cry. But Mom said I was pretty, although I never believed it.

But my sister Marla was pretty, and sometimes I was jealous. I could talk her into giving me anything she had. It was so easy. She always had the prettiest doll, and she always traded me for my doll that I didn't like. And then I would feel bad.

She loved Sam and would come running to him whenever he came into the house crying "Sabit" because she couldn't pronounce his name.

When Dad drank, he was like a wild animal. Mom had to look at us twice through black and blue eyes. She looked like a raccoon. Once, he even broke her nose. When he took her to the doctor, Dad told him that Mom had "banged into a door." The doctor didn't believe it.

"Are you trying to kill her?" he asked and told Mom to leave him.

I remember we were always at the police station. They told her to leave too. Sometimes she did. Sometimes she just couldn't take it.

But it wasn't all bad. Dad loved Italian food, and he liked to take us for spaghetti and meatballs at the Larga Roma tavern. We were happy then. We liked it when he sang to us too. He would sing us songs about his "bronco" that threw him and The Strawberry Roan. We didn't know his "bronco" was his motorcycle. And Mom would laugh.

Every time my mother left him, she took us to my grandparents' house. Granny and Pepere didn't mind. But Dad would always come to her and beg for forgiveness. Once, he grabbed my sister and kidnapped her. It was part of a plan to get Mom back. He left my sister with his mother and, the next day, went to tell my mother.

"Marla has swallowed a pin! You've got to come home to take care of her. She needs you. Please, come back. I need you too. I'm sorry. I won't do it again. I love you."

She went back more times than I can count. Once, my uncle Jeffrey, Dad's brother, came to see Mom and talked her into going back to him.

"If it doesn't work out this time, I'll never ask you again," he promised.

But it didn't work because my mother was suspicious of my father. Whenever Dad didn't come straight home from work, she questioned him over and over. One day she broke the window screen in her bedroom when she tried to see if he was parking with another woman in front of the house.

He had never cheated on her, but it made him very angry to think that she suspected him. One night she left us alone and walked to the barroom where Dad always went. She sneaked inside and, when she saw him talking to a woman, she was so angry she chased her into the ladies' room, pounded on the door, and started swearing at her.

"You're trying to steal my husband!" she screamed.

Dad made her go outside, and he gave her the beating of her life.

That night she packed a few things in a small red wagon and took us to Granny's house. My sister, younger brother, and I couldn't walk very far, so she put us in the wagon. Sam had to walk. He always had to do "grownup" things. My sister was scared stiff, and I was all mixed up. I couldn't figure out anything—didn't know why all these things were happening. Jack Junior was probably mixed up too.

My mother looked like raw hamburger when she showed up at my grandparents' house.

My brother Sam was a very serious child. Mom used to brag about him being able to say the alphabet by heart before he was two. He sure was the smartest one, and he sailed through grammar school at the top of the class. And he was the biggest. He had brown eyes and brown hair like Mom.

He was almost eight at the time my parents separated. Being the eldest, he was our protector, and he was happy that Dad didn't live with us anymore.

I had terrible nightmares after that. One nightmare was about a big spider that was on the ceiling just over my head. In my dream I had to lay there as he slowly came down a string he made. He always came to within a few inches of my face. When he reached the bottom, he would jump up to the top, and would start all over again. The suspense was horrible.

Jack Junior was the active one, and he always had a shy smile. He hated school, but he went every day anyway. He never stayed in the house. Each year he slept outside on the porch from March to November, even when there was snow on his blankets. He was either swimming or camping or climbing all the time, and he never sat still. Mom said Jack Junior and I were worms because we always wiggled.

Marla was scared of everything. During a thunderstorm, she went nuts. She would run around the house, screaming and crying, and then she'd hide herself in a closet.

She was afraid of Dad. She never wanted to come to him when he came over for visits. Her face was chubby and adorable, and her red hair was curly like Dad's. She was always trying to scrub off her freckles. And she could still be talked into anything.

Mom never wanted a divorce because she was Roman Catholic, but Dad would hear of nothing else. So when all the kids had mothers and fathers who lived together, we were a "divorced" family.

. . .

"You don't belong here. This is not your house," my old maid aunt Sarah would yell at us when we got out of hand, which was often. I got so sick of her telling us it wasn't our house.

Even though she had the biggest brightest room in the house, she was jealous of Mom and us because she had to share the house with us. She had wanted it for herself. Life had been cruel to her. Everyone said she was "slow."

As a child she woke up more than once in the middle of the night and found herself sitting on her neighbor's porch with her feet in the snow. She started to shiver in her thin nightgown and began to cry. Her cries awoke her neighbor who let her inside and gave her a hot cup of tea.

And when she was fourteen until she turned eighteen, she was committed to a mental institution.

My grandmother always said that she was sick because she fell into a tub of bluing water when she was very young. But we didn't understand why she could be so cruel.

"I want peace and quiet," she would shout. "Who do you think you are anyway? You belong on the streets."

We fought often and played tricks on Granny. She wore many petticoats under her housedress, and we would sneak behind her and place a "kick me" sign on the back of her dress. Granny thought it was funny; Auntie Sarah never did.

We'd play "water tag" in the summer. We'd run around the house with glasses of water, trying to get the "bad guy." There was water all over the place, even on the window screens, because we'd play outside as well as inside and hurl the water through the windows. It was cool and fun.

Samuel would hang his long johns on a broomstick over the stairway and make a puppet out of them by tying strings to the legs. Granny would laugh so hard her belly would shake.

Our Granny was very old, sixty-five when Mom came home with us. And she was the backbone of our family at that time— mine anyway. When a nightmare would haunt me, and I ran to her big feather bed, I'd be able to sleep soundly.

We had oodles of cousins because she had thirteen children. And she made the money stretch. We had more vegetables than most people because she grew corn, beans, lettuce, tomatoes, radishes, and so many vegetables I can't remember in her small garden.

But I remember the strawberry patch because I loved strawberries. And the rhubarb. We used to put sugar in whiskey glasses and take them out into the garden. Then we'd peel the rhubarb and dip them in sugar. It was so good.

It was a very old two-story house that had formerly been a barn, and every piece of furniture in it was broken, as well as every spoke on the stairs. The rooms were small, except for Aunt Sarah's room which stretched across the entire front of the house. We had one bathroom with a tub, sink, and toilet, with no hot water. Taking a bath was a real challenge.

Even though the house was very cold, and we couldn't afford to have a glass of milk or orange juice whenever we wanted it, I felt I was very rich because of Granny's garden and the woods at the back of the house and in front of the house.

One night, while Mom was working the second shift, we got on Sarah's nerves again.

"Get out!" she screamed at us as she flung open the kitchen door. Then, she kicked us out one by one into the night. "I can't stand you anymore."

Her actions made no sense to us because, this time, we had been busy studying for school. This time we had been quiet. We had been completely taken by surprise.

Sam carried Marla, who had no shoes on, through our neighbor's junkyard so she wouldn't cut her feet on splintered glass that he knew was scattered on the ground. She held on as tightly as she could to his hand. That night we slept in a nearby barn. We could smell the barn smells: urine, dung, and the mold of old textile leavings. While we lay on rags, Samuel promised, "When I get big, I'll get a job, and we'll get our own house. I'll take care of Ma and us. Don't worry."

. . .

Dad was not the same after the divorce. Although he never sought treatment for his problem, he often found himself running down the streets with tears in his eyes, plagued by feelings of loss and guilt. He thought about suicide. My Uncle Jeffrey, his brother, had to sleep with him many nights to prevent this from happening.

Finally, his brother Louie sent him a telegram which read, "Jack, come stay with me in Missouri for a rest."

Dad hopped on his motorcycle and headed west. He spent several months there and met Lucy. She was the type of woman he had always needed, someone who was slow to anger, someone who understood the fact that he had emotional problems. She gave him reason to live and love again. And when the divorce was final, they returned to Rhode Island and got married.

. . .

Dad never forgot us. At Christmas time, he would arrive with a pickup truck full of toys that Lu had carefully wrapped herself. Sam got the lion's share, and Dad always called him his "big boy."

"Come here, Samuel. The scooter is yours. Do you like the new desk? I even got you a school box. I know you'll share."

Then he'd call me over and call me his "big girl." Jack Junior was his "little boy," and Marla, of course, was the "little girl."

I always noticed that his hands shook, and he never stayed long. I still couldn't understand the whole thing, but I knew I was hurt.

We snatched up the toys and games anyway, wishing we had a father on Christmas like other children.

Mom always stayed in the background, wishing she had the money to buy those toys herself but happy that her children were having fun. She wasn't sorry about the divorce though.

She was happy it was over. She wasn't jealous anymore. I was the one who was jealous of my new stepmother. When Dad remarried, I felt betrayed again.

Granny always stood in the doorway, glaring at Dad until he left.

While the three of us would come to our father, Marla held back. She always stood like a lifeless rag doll in a corner, her hand clutching Mom's skirts. Whenever Dad made an attempt to get close to her, she backed away.

CHAPTER 2

"**C**'mon, Sam, play ball."

"Okay, but my sister will have to play too. It's touch football. I won't let you tackle her."

My brother bellowed out the commands, and soon I could feel the ball whiz over my head. William John, Ed Tremer, and the others always agreed, although they didn't especially like the idea of playing football with a girl. Even in the excitement of the game, I rarely missed the ball when he threw it to me. He let me kick as well, although I had to take my shoe off to make the ball go any distance at all. He was my brother, my hero.

I also admired him for other reasons. He spent hours making intricate airplane models out of tissue paper and balsa wood. Every piece had to be perfect, and every piece had to fit just so. An owner of a neighborhood store wanted to display one model in his store window. Nevertheless, Sam refused. He smashed every one of his delicate models soon after he made them.

His mind was always open to some new challenge, one of which was being a theater director. The stage always was in the junkyard next door, where he could find plenty of space and props. They were action plays, sometimes about cowboys and Indians and sometimes about Tarzan of the Apes, but the plots were similar: strong tough guy rescues fair maiden.

For the Tarzan plays, I usually played the part of Jane, and the boy next door, Edgar, played Tarzan. Jack Junior played the part of Cheetah, a chimpanzee, and Sam and David Marlow played the bad guys who would kidnap me, upon which time he would tell me to scream as loud as I could to make it convincing. He charged six cents for admission. Mom, Edgar's parents, Granny, and even Aunt Sarah were most often the audience.

Another time he made several carts and formed a parade which marched down the small country road where we lived. He pounded on a tin pail with a wooden spoon which he had found. Edgar scraped an old screen with a rusty spatula. My younger brother was always a part of the fun, riding in one of the carts Sam and he had made out of rusty wheels and secondhand lumber.

This was quite an event on the street where we lived called Allens Avenue, which made Mr. Gray, who owned the house next door, chuckle. Samuel was the guy who was going to make a difference in our lives and the lives of others, and he taught us so much in the small space of time he was with us.

He was an expert swimmer, and he loved to impress his girlfriend with his long, powerful strokes when he, Jack Junior, and Marla were swimming at New River in Central Falls, Rhode Island.

Al, Jack Junior, and I played in the junkyard most of the time. It wasn't a junkyard to us. It was our paradise, a place that held adventure, a place where we could create. Textile spools became ice cream cones. The old well held water that would flood the little imaginary villages we had made out of pieces of wood, and our tiny people always escaped in miniature boats, probably bottle caps, that were tied up near their houses.

It wasn't the same with my sister. Marla had her fears that seemed to grow with her. Whenever a thunderstorm took place, she would run into the house, screaming and cringing in terror with her hands clamped over her ears.

"The thunder is going to get me!"

Then she'd shut herself in the closet in the upstairs hallway.

She also rocked so hard in bed that the hair on the back of her head would snarl in a big ball. And we'd laugh at her. Granny couldn't comb it out, and she'd have to go to school looking like a giant Brillo pad. But she really never cared what she looked like because she knew she could get away with anything if she smiled. Besides, she often poked fun at us too.

"This is the way Mom walks."

She'd giggle as she would turn over on her ankles. At the same time she would knock her knees together and warble like a duck across the floor.

"And this is Aunt Sarah," she would squeal as she put wax fruit under her sweater. Then she'd arch her back and parade around with the fruit bouncing. We would burst with laughter at those hilarious antics.

Mom smiled more often. She taught me how to dance the waltz, jitterbug, fox trot, the polka, and even how to tap dance. The polka was her favorite. We often went out together to the Polish American Hall on Benefit Street in Pawtucket to dance where her brother Edward had his band. I was tall, so I fit into Mom's dresses except for the bosom part, which I stuffed with old socks. She even won a bottle of wine for her rendition of "Who's Sorry Now."

One night, while she was singing, she spotted a young man standing in a far corner.

"Who is that guy in khakis?" she whispered to Edward.

"Don't you remember Raymond Perez?" he reminded her. "You used to have a crush on him in high school."

Her eyes sparkled when she recalled her feelings for a handsome boy so long ago.

Raymond had been staring at her for the good part of the evening, and their eyes had exchanged glances several times.

"Was that the same pest he had tried to get rid of—the little girl, Edward's kid sister, who was always peeping around the corner when he was practicing his violin with Edward?"

He knew he had to ask her for a date, and he did before the night was over. He was now a World War II private who had earned the Purple Heart for the frostbite that had plagued him during German winters. He had come home on furlough to spend time with his family in Attleboro, Massachusetts.

It felt strange for me to have a mother who was dating, but everyone was happy about that, especially Mom. Even Granny enjoyed having a glass of her "home brew" with him.

One day in 1946, before Raymond returned to Germany for five months to complete his tour, my mother called me into the bedroom and informed me she was thinking of marriage. I was puzzled. Why did she have to tell me? I figured it was because she thought I was smart, even though I was ten.

She went on, "If you don't want me to, I won't."

I thought it over. Raymond was good to us kids. And he loved Mom. I could tell. It would be great to have a father around the house like my friends did. I gave my approval, and Mom gave her promise to him.

What could she lose? She would have a companion, someone to help her with the children and the bills. Also, we knew her job working in a defense plant for the war effort and the good-sized pay check would be over when the boys came home. She would have to pack away her bib- overalls and Thermos like millions of other women and bid goodbye to big machines, lathes, and shells.

. . .

The day of the wedding ceremony he got stoned, and afterward, he moved into Granny's house with us. The familiar smell of alcohol always filled the kitchen when he played cards with us and showed us tricks with his cigarettes. I thought his red eyeballs were a sign that he needed glasses, but I didn't want to hurt his feelings by telling him so.

One day, he came home carrying a case of beer with a roll of $20 bills sticking out of his breast pocket. Then he set down the beer and held out the money.

"Hi, ya, Runt (the name he had given my mother), here have a glass of beer. I bought a case. See all this money? I sold the truck. Why worry about money?"

He was drooling from the corners of his mouth, and he spilled beer down the front of his faded shirt.

"Oops," he laughed and tripped over his own feet.

We knew then we were in for big trouble because the truck had been all he owned. His father had given it to him to start a small business with. After that day, I began to witness our happy family go through a period of degradation unlike it had ever been before. We began to attend Alcoholics Anonymous and Sam Anon meetings for families of alcoholics, as Mom tried desperately to save her marriage. And she made as many friends as she could with other wives of alcoholics. Her closest friend from AA was a lady named "Fritzie," who was always visiting our home trying to encourage my mother. Raymond refused to believe that he was ill and wouldn't go to the meetings with us nor talk to other former alcoholics.

Nothing worked. He began stealing money from her pocketbook after that, and he even came into my bedroom once and took my piggybank. It was a maroon piggybank in the shape of a dollar sign with a drawer on the bottom that sprung open to reveal the money. I had over $16 in that bank. From then on, I felt guilty for telling my mother to marry him and for all the other things that happened thereafter.

That's when I first had a glimpse of the fiend, and he brought dread to my heart when he began nibbling at my brother. Nobody had paid any attention to Sam until his screams of agony woke us on Christmas night. He was doubled over with pains in his abdomen, and Mom rushed him to Chapan Memorial Hospital in Rhode Island. The doctors were puzzled, so they ordered many tests. Eventually, they diagnosed rheumatic fever and sent him home after a two-week stay. He spent two and a half weeks in bed, screeching and raging with horrible nightmares. His delirium was so bad Mom had to sleep with him. His eyes were glazed, and he claimed to see the devil at night.

"He's tempting me, Ma!" he would yell in the small hours of the morning. "Make him go away."

His eyes would roll around to the back of his head, and he would clutch his fists. We had heard of the Devil in catechism, but to have him in the house with us was frightening.

Then, as suddenly as the illness came, it also left. To our amazement, he seemed to recover. The fever was gone and the Devil with it. Still, Samuel was never the same. The old sparkle was gone. I watched it happen. It was apparent that he was not happy anymore, and to make matters worse, he had a pizza face. He began to fail in school and seemed to care little about what was going on around him.

Except for germs. When we sat down for dinner, no one could move, or germs might fall on his plate. He washed his utensils over and over and covered his food. We couldn't relax until he left the table. We used to kid him about the germs, but then he would get angry. Since he was the strongest person in the house, we had reason to fear his anger. Explaining did no good. He wouldn't listen. Everything with him was germs, germs, germs.

But Mom was content that he was well. Besides, Raymond took center stage again after Sam recovered from the fever. He decided to be jealous of her. It didn't matter what she did or where she went, she was cheating on him. When she went to the store, she was cheating on him. When she went to work, she was cheating on him. And she didn't dare go visiting. Finally, his demented mind devised a plan.

"I'll show her."

He grabbed the razor with shaking hands. As he moved the blade up and down across his wrists, he made the cut. It was not deep enough to do him any real damage but deep enough to impress Mom.

"Aah."

Mom could hear the forced moan from downstairs in the kitchen, where she was working. When she found him in a pool of blood (albeit a small pool), she called the rescue squad. This he had not counted on.

"My husband is bleeding to death!"

She grabbed clean rags and held them on the wounds until the ambulance arrived.

"No!" he shouted. "I don't wanna go. Leave me alone."

"But, Mr. Perez, you're bleeding quite a bit. At least let us stop the bleeding," the medic said. "You may get infected."

But Raymond had accomplished his purpose. He had already caused my mother a great deal of anguish, and when the van pulled out of the yard, I could see him grinning behind his raised elbow.

Another time, a bottle of aspirin tablets "accidentally" got flushed down the toilet. Again the rescue squad arrived at our house.

We were convinced that he really meant to do it each time and lived in fear of the sound of a siren. Ambulances must have made a path from driving back and forth to our house.

As time went on though, the threat of suicide wasn't having a big impact on us anymore. We accepted it as part of our daily routine. Still, I was in for another big surprise. I first became aware of it when Mom took me to the train station in Providence to ask about the cost of tickets to the West Coast.

"We must get away, Ruth, as far away as possible before he kills me. We'll send for the other kids when we get there."

This sent me into a panic. What was she talking about? I had noticed her crying and had seen the pounds disappear from her body, but I never fully understood why until now.

I decided to take action, so I took her to the "bug house" (otherwise known as the Broadway Theater) to get her mind off her troubles.

It worked. Mom and I came home from the show making jokes about the bugs in the bug house. When we opened the door to the house, however, Aunt Sarah was waiting for us with a wide-eyed look of fear in her eyes. Raymond had been there with a gun.

We were upstairs in the bedroom, trying to decide what to do when she yelled, "Hide! He's coming down the walk. I'll try to get rid of him."

Mom and I hid under our bed. I was quivering so badly that the bed shook.

Surely he'll see it moving. I could hear heavy footsteps climbing the stairs, and the odor of beer was everywhere. A fly landed on my nose, and I was afraid to move, so I let it tickle me.

"Where's Leslie?"

We could hear the rifle click as he cocked it. I sucked in my breath. If I held it long enough maybe he wouldn't hear me breathing. I saw tears trickle down my mother's face and reached for her hand.

"I dunno. She's gone. She's not here."

We hoped he would be satisfied with her answer and dared not think of what might happen if he wasn't, but he headed for the bedroom. I had not noticed the squeak on the floor before but will never forget the sound of it as my mother and I lay paralyzed under the bed, and my stepfather paraded around the room.

He finally went out the door and stumbled down the stairs. He left. And mom threw up. We stayed in the house after that with Sarah as our "lookout," afraid to leave and afraid to stay.

We didn't have to wait long, however. Later on that day we heard a bulletin over the radio.

"A man held up and robbed the Cumberland Farms store in Pawtucket on Broadway near Benefit Street this afternoon. The man was apprehended shortly afterward and is now in police custody.

The police spotted the suspicious-looking character on Broadway immediately following the incident not far from the scene of the crime and arrested him."

We knew it was Raymond, and I was relieved. But Mom was convinced she wasn't safe, would never be safe again. He was going to get out someday and kill her. She knew this for certain. And no matter how many times she washed the walls or the sink or scrubbed the cupboards, no matter how much ironing she did, she knew someday he was going to walk into that house with a gun or a knife and kill her.

She wore the telltale frown of worry and tear-filled eyes day and night, and she wasn't interested in keeping herself bathed and pretty. She looked old and tired, and because she couldn't operate the foot press when her mind was not clear, she asked for time off and admitted herself into Foxboro Mental Hospital in Foxboro, Massachusetts.

Her condition was so severe that her doctors ordered electroshock treatments. She screamed in horror when they forced electric currents into her brain until her body could take no more. The terrible kind-cruelty changed her life forever.

Mom wrote to me every day, and I could tell by the jagged letters that she was tormented inside. I didn't know what to do. Night after night, I sat on Mr. Gray's stone wall, looking at the sky for answers. I could no longer believe in God, and even if there was a God, he was up there having a good laugh. I knew only one thing for certain: there was a monster in our midst, and he was clutching at all of us, even me. And I was fighting a losing battle.

Finally, the doctors realized the shock treatments weren't being effective. She had to confront her husband. It was her only chance for recovery. They contacted Raymond's mother. Because her husband had been a councilor for the town of Attleboro, she used his influence to have her son released from jail. Then she spoke to Raymond.

"You made her sick. Now you're going to make her well."

"It's not my fault," Raymond insisted. "It was the war that did this to me. Can't you see?"

"It's about time you take responsibility for your actions. She's a good woman, and I'm not going to let you hurt her anymore. You either go to that hospital or you go back to jail."

Raymond went to Foxboro to talk to my mother, and she came home two weeks later, damaged. Part of her memory was gone, and what she had left was not clear.

I gave in to the monster shortly afterward, and when he came, I didn't recognize him. I was walking down the stairs when my legs turned to jelly. Then, I tumbled over and over until I crumbled into a ball at the bottom on the stairs. I began to scream in terror.

"My legs! I can't move my legs. What's happening to me? Someone, help!"

My grandmother found me there, picked me up, and rubbed Omega oil (her cure for everything) on my legs. It worked. For a while. At times my legs would function, and at times I couldn't control them. When my girlfriend Jane came over for a visit, she told me that her father could help me. After all, he was a doctor who had a certificate on his wall that proved he had graduated from a six-month correspondence course he had taken, and the sign he displayed on his house with the long word printed on it (that I couldn't pronounce) impressed me.

My mother wasn't impressed though, so I agreed to see him against her wishes, and after a brief examination, he gave me his diagnosis.

"You have blood clots in your intestines, and you'll die if I don't treat you."

I was horrified and hurried home to tell Mom.

"Mr. Leland is no real doctor," she said. "Try some more Omega oil."

I didn't want to die, and I was desperate. I had no job at fourteen and could see no way of paying for treatments. But the Omega oil wore off, and Granny could tell that I needed more than Omega oil to cure me. That's when Aunt Sarah offered to help. She was the only one in the family who owned a car. It was an old Buick, and she was very possessive of it. No one had ever been allowed to ride in, sit in, or even touch it until now. I was fortunate. I think it was because she got tired of hearing me wailing about not wanting to die. At any rate, she drove me to my father's house.

"You'd better help your daughter. She's your responsibility, you know."

With that, she left.

Dad had always been there for us. Yet when he had heard that Mom was in the hospital, he was reluctant to give his child support payments to Granny because the battle between them had festered for years. Instead, he had taken the four of us shopping for new clothes for school. The clothes were to compensate for the child support. Granny didn't like that, of course, and she took him to court, where he lost the battle. The judge placed him on probation for seven years.

And here I was again on my father's doorstep anyway, looking for a handout. Again, Dad didn't let me down.

Of course, Dad ruled out Dr. Leland's diagnosis, but he did take me to a diagnostician, who tested every part of my body. I got the full treatment: heart, lungs, blood pressure, eyes, ears. The doctor paid special attention to my intestines and reflexes. He even had a row of bottles in his lab and made me sniff four or five of them. Then he had me look into a small telescope, and he instructed me to match my blood sample with others.

When he showed me the results he said, "Your blood is as rich as a construction worker's."

His diagnosis hit me like a thunderbolt. "You're as healthy as an old cow, but you have the nerves of a sixty-three-year-old woman."

I was so relieved I could've cried. I wasn't going to die. No one I knew of had died from nerves.

Then he looked at my father.

"You may want to take this young lady to a psychiatrist. I recommend Dr. Mongello. He's good in situations of this kind."

Dad was relieved too and agreed. In two weeks he took me to Dr. Mongello's office. It was the first time I had been in a mansion, and the splendor of the structure intrigued me. The house was over two hundred years old, and a circular stairway with a mahogany railing and carved spindles greeted us at the door. The furniture was equally impressive, although not comfortable.

The doctor was a very soft-spoken person, and he put me at ease immediately. He wanted me to tell him my life's story. I answered all of his questions, and he suggested that I leave my environment and stay with my father for a while.

"Ruth," he advised, "you can't be worrying about everyone in your family. I want you to forget your family and think of yourself. You're young and healthy, and you have your whole lifetime ahead of you. Enjoy it."

Then he wanted to talk to Dad and asked me to leave the room. I could hear him yelling at my father through the closed door.

"Do you realize what you did to this child? Now it's up to you to become the father you should've been right from the start."

Dad had already spent $70 to find out what was wrong with me, and he couldn't afford a doctor who yelled at him and blamed him for things that had happened in the past. He now had four young children with my stepmother and had to support them as well.

And I no longer worried about my family nor my health. I didn't need a doctor, and I didn't want one. So I deserted my sister when she needed me the most. I went to live with Dad. Samuel was becoming more and more violent each day, and she lived in fear of him.

Something else happened shortly after I left, which I was not aware of until years later. Edgar coerced her to go with him into the cellar of Granny's house one day when Samuel and Jack Junior were not present.

"Come on, Marla. Don't be afraid. I have something nice to show you."

Not knowing what to expect, she had gone with him. Then he put his hands under her panties and aroused feelings in her she had never experienced before.

"Now don't tell your mother," he told her when it was over. "Promise?"

"Promise."

She told anyway, but Mom didn't think it was important. After all, it was a sin to talk about sex in those days, and her mother had never told her anything either.

"Have nothing to do with him. He's a bad boy," she said.

Marla stayed closer to Mom after that. She began to shun boys because she felt dirty, and she became more withdrawn. She was afraid of growing up, afraid of heights, of loud noises, of people, of elevators, afraid to take responsibility—afraid of everything, until her fears reached epidemic proportions.

She also didn't want to do anything. She never washed a dish, cleaned the house, nor took care of her own clothes. Granny did the cooking, and Mom did the rest. In fact, she only wanted to stay in the comfort and security of her bed permanently and totally. And the fear eventually led to anger, which began to swell inside her. Of course, she took it out on Mom, who was the only person within reach of her pent-up feelings, and the only one who would let her get away with it.

"Ma, make me a sandwich."

"Would you like the leftover meat pie in the ice box?"

"No, I want a sandwich. You heard me."

This became the pattern of her whole life from then on, a life of humiliation, despair, and hopelessness, and none of us were able to decipher what was happening inside her head or to foresee its ramifications.

While I was recovering from my bout with the monster, I visited Mom, my brothers, and my sister often. I was anxious to permanently return to my original family because I felt more comfortable with them. Even so, once in South Attleboro, I discovered that I missed my stepmother and my aunt and the chats we used to have about grownup things and faraway places.

Besides, life with my mother and Raymond was still very tense. He was drinking heavily. One day, when I saw him shove Mom onto the parlor couch, I attacked him.

"This time I'm not merely a victim, I thought. This time I can do something about it."

I picked up every book in the World Book Encyclopedia set and threw them all at him. In his drunken stupor, he was no match for my fury. He retreated to his bedroom where he could sleep it off.

The next day, when he came home from the barroom, he found that I had stuffed his clothes in paper grocery bags and left them on the front porch. I had bolted the door.

He pounded on the door with his fists and yelled, "Let me in. I live here, you know."

No one answered his cries. After a few hours, he took his things and left. From that day on, he lived on the streets, disowned by his family and society.

. . .

Lucy laughed at the sight of me.

"I don't know how you walk those hot railroad tracks with no shoes on. Your feet must be as tough as shoe leather. Are you hungry?" she asked.

I nodded.

"Come on in. I'll heat up a can of soup for you and make you a sandwich."

She was a terrific person—kind, caring, and she loved us even though we weren't her own. Still, her younger sister Sherry, who was married to Dad's younger brother, was smarter, prettier, and tougher. The two couples lived in Uncle Jeffrey's house.

One day, Auntie Sherry and Uncle Jeffrey took me to Lincoln Amusement Park in Massachusetts, and because they knew I was eager to go on the rides and was too young to go unless I was accompanied by an adult, my uncle went with me. And when the bullets we were riding on went upside down, he almost squashed me when he came crashing down on top of me.

He laughed so hard I thought his huge belly would bust, and I'm sure everyone in the park heard us howl when the cover of the caterpillar covered us and we were wrenched around in the dark. Auntie Sherry was thrilled and excited for me. Without the two of us, I believe her day would have been boring.

No ride was out of my reach. For me, it was a day of total abandonment to fun.

Most of the time though, Sherry was a serious person. She was well-read, and she was interested in me. We talked endlessly about my future and life in general. No one had ever given me this much attention before, and I basked in the warm glow of her affection and that of her husband's. At that time I had no inclination of how they would affect my destiny.

CHAPTER 3

"Hey, Rip Van Winkle, are you going to sleep your way through class again?"

Ping. A spitball hit Samuel on the back of his head. He tensed. A muscle on his arm pulsed, but he said nothing. His dark eyes stared straight ahead. One of the teenagers strolled past him, spit in his direction, and laughed. Samuel sat motionless, and his face betrayed feelings of helplessness. The cruelty continued relentlessly, day after day, until he could take no more.

Although I had noticed he had stopped going to school and was letting his appearance become sloppy, unfortunately I was unable to interpret these as signs that the monster was trying to take hold again. I told my father that he was becoming lazy, hoping that he could talk some sense into him. Because I was late to see the battle my brother was engaged in, I betrayed him, and I will never forgive myself for it. My father's lecture was ineffective anyway. Sam didn't seem to care anymore.

But I was unwilling to accept this. Determined to make him go back myself, I begged him, "One more time, Sam, for me?"

He had been taught to be big and strong, and he was doing his best to follow those instructions. Like a wounded soldier, he was dragging himself up to the top of the hill, facing a barrage of enemy fire. No matter what the danger, he had to try. Maybe one last rigorous effort would prove successful.

That day, I took the school bus home late. This time I was witness to the taunting and the agony he was suffering, and I tried to defend him on the bus by yelling at the hoodlums and showing my fists. They only laughed and told him he was hiding behind his sister's skirts. I realized then I had only made matters worse.

When we reached our stop, he bolted from the bus, ran as fast as he could to our house, and locked himself in his room. I followed him, feeling helpless, and stood outside of his bedroom door, listening to him sob.

"I won't ask you to do it again, Sam. I'm sorry."

After that, the once proud and talented child who had been the neighborhood chess champion quit school. When a kind man gave him a job working on a garbage truck, he found that he couldn't handle it because he could not remember which yard he was to go to next. Reluctantly the man fired him.

Soon afterward, a young priest noticed him crying in church. Samuel was carrying a Bible, pointing to passages and reading them aloud. The concerned priest paid my mother a visit.

"I have a brother like Samuel," he told her. "I know how to help him. Let me put him in Cumberland Hills Monastery where someone can watch over him. He's a good boy."

"Oh, no!" Mom was indignant. "I won't let him leave home. He's too young."

"But he needs guidance now. It's not wise to wait."

Her stubbornness would not budge.

The priest sadly shook his head and left. I'm sure Samuel was in his prayers often after that.

Before the year was over, Samuel rammed himself through the window of his second-floor bedroom. Glass, wood, and screen came crashing down on top of him, as the pitiful sixteen-year-old child tried desperately to end the life that had become unbearable to him.

He lay there, unable to move, until Mom, Granny, and Aunt Sarah, who were awakened by the crash at four o'clock in the morning, brought him into the house. His body was covered with blood and bruises, and he was begging Mom to take him to see a psychiatrist and saying something incomprehensible about the little fishes. Concerned about these little fishes, he never noticed that a nail had pierced his own foot.

Mom rushed to the neighbor's house and called Dad and an ambulance, but when they arrived, Sam didn't want to go. He put up quite a fight, punching and kicking in all directions while three strong men, including my father, wrestled with him and put him in a straitjacket.

Then he became silent, showing no sign of emotion. They took him to the Institute of Mental Health in Providence. Dad hired the best psychiatrists that he could buy, but they held no hope for his recovery. Without communication with him, treatment was impossible. Samuel couldn't come out of a mind that had become a cage to him and talk to anyone. His doctors diagnosed schizophrenia, a term I grew to hate and fear more each day. The demon now had a name.

Dad, Lucy, Aunt Sherry, and Uncle Jeffrey sheltered me from the horrors that were happening to my brother. They told me nothing about it at first, and when they did, the pain I felt hurt so bad it seemed to get stuck in my chest, and I was unable to cry. They also encouraged me to focus on other things. I liked school, and I found refuge in books.

I had always been curious. As a child I had always looked at the sky with wonder. I had even chosen a star all my own. It was a seemingly insignificant star in the heavens, but when I gave her a name, it seemed to make me a part of the universe. Surely, someone or something greater than us masterminded creation.

I used to take the longer walk home from school, which led through the woods, so I could smell the wild flowers and put my bare feet into the icy cold water of the brook that seemed to come from nowhere and cascade down the rocks to form a small pond below. Tiny tadpoles always wiggled in my hands until I would let them go. I wondered where they came from and how they got there. The maple, oak, ash, and birch trees brought me the most delight though, especially in the autumn with their crimson and yellow and purple and orange hues. The forest seemed to comfort and to caress me.

Now my curiosity led me to black print on white pages. I devoured all the information I could about anything and everything. It had begun with fairytales, poetry, especially Edgar Alan Poe and Walt Whitman and some literature, although I confess I didn't quite understand Shakespeare. Then mythology grabbed my attention. Why did all those ancient peoples concoct such intricate beliefs, and was any of it true? Certainly some of it all seemed to be related somehow.

The germ of a quest began to develop inside of me that I didn't fully understand. I commenced a search in order to answer all the many questions that I so desperately asked myself. Why did all this have to happen to my family? Could there be a God? Was there any chance for Sam to recover? Were there other people who had this illness? Would Marla end up in a hospital too? I needed to know the answers.

It is a passion that continues to this day. When Sherry's sister Pink piqued my interest in the Bible, I began to search the Scriptures. I studied for long periods of time, often all night, which aroused my Aunt Sherry's curiosity. She studied with me. I found some of the answers to my questions in the pages of this marvelous book.

Finally, gradually, faith came to me, and God has sustained me through all the ordeals and afflictions that I have had to face in my life. I also believe that my faith has kept me from going crazy, although I found out many years later that I was, am, and always will be an insane person. His love filled all the empty corners I seemed to have in my heart, and I no longer blame him for the evil in this world. Sometimes man himself is responsible.

I also discovered that God performs miracles every day, and the biggest miracles happen inside of us. When I became a born-again Christian, amazingly, so did my father, stepmother, aunt, and uncle. That Christmas, Bibles were the biggest and most expensive gifts under the tree.

Together we joined a small white church with a tiny steeple, and Dad stood in front of the congregation with tears streaming from his pale blue eyes, his body trembling, and confessed his sins. This was something he had decided to do himself. No one had expected it to happen. He told of the things he did to my mother, and he told of the things he had done to us kids. It seemed to make it easier for him to forgive himself.

My mother struggled on. The pain she was bearing inside was taking its toll. She looked older and more serious, and she didn't laugh much anymore, although she did make a futile effort at humor whenever she could. Even though her youthful appearance had left her long ago, men still found her attractive. She was stunning with her sable hair rolled back that displayed her widow's peak.

When I turned sixteen, I went shopping in Peerless in Pawtucket—the most expensive store I knew of—and bought Mom a beautiful black velvet fitted suit. Mom looked lovely in black. Besides, she was worth it. She took it back the next day, got a refund, and bought clothes for us four kids.

That hurt my feelings, but I did finally manage to make her something she loved. I found some blue-and-white checkered cotton material in Granny's sewing drawer and made her a wraparound housedress which she hardly ever took off. She wore it every day after work. She was definitely not interested in another marriage.

Her attention now focused on my brother. Even in the most terrible snowstorms, she wouldn't miss a week of visiting him in the hospital. She had no finances available to purchase an automobile, and she had no driver's license, so she made the trip every Sunday, toting a bag of clothes and food with her.

She also pleaded with doctors to let Sam come home as often as possible, which proved to be successful frequently, although it probably wasn't the wisest thing to do. He didn't know who he was anymore. Still, he always recognized Mom when he saw her. His illness caused him to have fits of violence though. Once he grabbed a patient by the neck and wrestled him to the floor.

"I hate you. I'm going to kill you," he vowed.

Four attendants seized my brother and put him in a straitjacket again. The man's only crime was that he happened to look like my father. Dad was not allowed to visit his son after that. He cried when he heard the news, and he carried the pain within his heart for the rest of his life.

But Sam's doctor allayed my mother's fears.

"He'll never hurt you," he said. "He loves you very much."

Marla had reason to fear though, when he came home to visit. Because his protective instincts were always a part of his psyche, he went wild when he witnessed the hurt Marla was inflicting on Mom. Once, he chased her around the house, threatening to choke her. She was forced to remain in her room after that.

School was a total failure for her, and a friendship or love for a boy was now not within her reach. Neither was a high school diploma. She thought she was ugly because of a mild case of acne and a face that blushed too easily. Besides, she was convinced that she wasn't smart like her older sister because her grades were poor. It never occurred to her that the guidance director had placed her in classes she had no aptitude for nor interest in the subject matter. And when I left, she had no mentor. She was like a little bird with a broken wing, flapping aimlessly.

But she loved children, especially babies. A poor couple, Mr. and Mrs. Stuart, lived with their seven children on Turner Street, which was adjacent to Allens Avenue, and Marla would often take care of them. They couldn't afford a babysitter, and she was happy to come over and work for free. The children were usually dirty, which is natural for children, and she would take them to our house, wash them, and feed them and tell them all kinds of stories.

Many days, she looked like the Pied Piper, with her trail of kids following after her, her ponytail bouncing back and forth, and the trickle of her laughter always warned us that the house would soon be invaded by tiny bare feet.

As for me, I became a runaway and a vagabond. I left Mom and Marla in the dust without looking back. I left Mom to carry her burden alone, and her burden was heavy. Her sad eyes never complained though, except to let me know she didn't want me to join the United States Air Force, upon which time I informed her that Dad would sign the papers if she wouldn't.

At that point, I actually had created a substitute mother in my mind and in my heart, even though I didn't realize it. I thought Mom was naive, which she was, of course, and I had tried to share my Christian experience with her. It would have made things easier for her, but she remained stubborn and set in her ways. It was like I couldn't reach her. There was a wedge between us, something I didn't know how to deal with.

On the other hand, Sherry was world-wise, and she saw the yearning in my eyes for distant shores.

CHAPTER 4

I woke up in a cold sweat and sat upright in bed; my heart hammered with a force so loud I could hear it. That dreadful nightmare had haunted me again. In the dream, an enormous lion was stalking me. He would slowly walk down the path to the front door of Granny's house, looking neither to the right nor to the left. I could see his tendons and muscles move in perfect rhythm and feel his power.

Then fear would grip me, a fear that had its basis in something too deep for me to fathom. Then I would frantically barricade the doors and windows with chairs, tables, and other pieces of furniture or whatever I could get my hands on, trying desperately to keep him from getting in, and I would wake up terrified.

The strange thing about the dream though, was that it wasn't the lion's ripping teeth or claws that I was afraid of. It was his eyes. For a reason I could not understand, looking in those eyes would be like facing something worse than death, like looking into the bowels of hell.

Why the lion? I pondered over and over in my mind. There was something about the big cats that had always held a fascination for me because, although they were fierce, they still maintained an elegance of movement about them which is admirable. Did they in fact represent something I both admired and feared? And what dread did those eyes really hold? The dream happened so often that I dreaded going to sleep at night.

The dream vanished miraculously when I turned sixteen, and although I was subjected to the same environment and had the same genetic background that my sister and older brother had, outside of sleepless nights, I escaped any serious mental disorders.

I seemed to be unscathed by negative outside influences now. Everyone liked me; I never questioned that, although it continually amazed me. I had no idea at that stage of my life what was wrong with Sam, nor did I surmise that it could ever happen to me. Besides, I never associated nerve problems with insanity. Most importantly I discovered that, when left by myself, I was a happy person.

Along with books, I loved to listen to stories that my many aunts and uncles told, especially Uncle Jeffrey's stories. He often spoke of Uncle Samuel, his oldest brother. Samuel had an unusual way of making spending money. He used to dare people to ride on the back of his motorcycle, and if they could manage to hold on, he would give them fifty cents. But if they fell off, they had to give him five cents. When he found anyone to take him up on his dare, he would drive around in circles until that unfortunate individual would fall off.

Then there was the time that Samuel carried a piano up to the second floor of an apartment building singlehandedly. (I never quite believed this.)

Because Samuel's father, my paternal grandfather, abused my grandmother and their children, Samuel took off for Florida when he was very young and lived there for two years. He returned to wait for the opportunity to settle the score. The next time his father smashed his mother across the face, he gave him such a severe beating that the man lay on the floor, bloody and still. Then Samuel called the police.

"I've just killed my father," his strained voice grunted.

Before the patrolman arrived, however, this father regained consciousness, crawled out the door and never came back.

After that, whenever Samuel saw a worried frown on his mother's face, he said to her: "Ma, if I die, pluck out my eyeballs, place them in a glass of water, and tie a string to one of them. If you get lonely, pull on the string, and I'll wink at you."

Samuel's fascinating life was short though. One day, while driving down a winding road, he came around a curve at top speed and crashed into the back of a stalled automobile, imbedding a crank deep into his skull. An ambulance arrived too late to save his life. Although medics stopped the bleeding and rushed him to Memorial Hospital, his only hope for recovery was brain surgery. The operation was scheduled for the following day.

That night he sneaked out of the hospital, jumped over a fence, ran across the street where his family lived, awoke my uncle and my father, tousled their hair, tossed them up and down in the air, and hugged them. Then he knocked on his mother's door.

"Mom, I've come home for a good cup of coffee," he told her.

After sharing the whole experience with them, he jumped the fence again, waved goodbye, climbed into a hospital window, and my family never saw him alive again. He died the next day on the operating table.

Sometime later, my grandmother received a letter from a girl in Florida that was addressed to Samuel. The words in its pages were full of her longing for him and her anticipation for his swift return. True romances have an aura about them that no poet can fully portray.

There were other stories too that were rich in excitement to me. I wanted to go to the place they talked about and to meet the people they met. I wanted to see what was beyond Rhode Island. Every time an airplane would fly overhead or a train would whistle by, I wished I was on it. My mind was like a giant sponge which soaked up knowledge to no end. There was always more room for one more fact, one more story, or one more insight.

Also, taking a long, scrutinizing look at myself in the mirror had become a pastime to me at age fourteen. Being a beanpole was no longer a problem because curves began to develop on my body which both surprised and delighted me. I now had a great figure by my own admission, even though I wasn't as satisfied with my face. My eyes were too small and not very striking. The blue actually had flakes of green, brown, and gray, and the color changed with the surrounding colors of the room or the dress I was wearing, making me feel like a chameleon.

My nose was long and narrow with a slight hump. That distressed me because I had always thought that the perfect nose had a turned-up end on it. In fact, I spent an entire year in school pushing the tip of my nose up with my finger, hoping it would grow that way. It didn't, of course, and it took another year for the line I had formed across it to disappear.

I had a wide grin and crooked teeth, and when I smiled, I tried to hide my teeth with my hand. Eventually, I decided I was plain rather than ugly and gave up on all that fussing around. After all, I still had to live with my face, no matter what.

Also, the mixing and matching of hand-me-down clothes that I still was happy to get had provoked a latent artistic skill to evolve in me that eventually enhanced the quality of my life.

Aunt Sherry influenced my young mind at that point more than anything or anyone else. She was a high school graduate, well-read and wise, which was a rarity in a woman in her generation. In fact, in my ivory tower, I thought that she was the most intelligent person in the entire world. Sherry was my idol, the woman I wanted to be. For sure, she was the most intelligent person I had ever met.

She was miles ahead of Mom. Ever since the day I was saying the rosary and had asked Mom what a womb was and she didn't know, I didn't trust her to know anything else. I knew then I had outgrown her.

My father never influenced me too much either because I had a problem trying to decide whether or not I loved him. Even though he was always there for me, I still blamed him in part for the things he had done to Sam and Mom. Although he began to attend church and tried to reform, he still drank too much.

One time he came home drunk and began to chase Lu around the living room. What was particularly horrible was that she had my half sister Olga in her arms.

She was yelling, "Jack, the baby!"

I was standing in the kitchen across the room from the sink and had a glass of water in my hand when I saw her race by the door. The thought flashed through my mind, "Don't let him hurt her." A loud screech escaped from my mouth, and at the same time, I flung the glass across the room. It hit the sink and splattered into a million pieces. Then I ran out of the room, down the street, and down the railroad tracks. I didn't stop until I reached my mother's home. After that incident, Dad seemed to simmer down a little, at least in front of me.

It was Sherry that put the bug in my mind about the air force and gave me the goal I needed.

"If I were young, I'd take advantage of the traveling that the service offers," she would often remark. "I wished I had traveled more."

Also, Sherry had a happy marriage, and I wanted that for myself someday. But still she cautioned me: "Don't get married too young. You've plenty of time for that."

When I was entering puberty, she answered all the many questions I had about sex, and because of my Christian religion and my aunt's advice, I believed that sex was strictly "taboo" until marriage. I enjoyed dates and the company of boys in general though, preferring it to the company of girls.

Boys were definitely more exciting, especially George Briggs, my high school boyfriend who impressed me by the black convertible that he used when he came calling on me, proudly displaying the welded-in fenders, windshield, and the new canvas he had placed on the top. What George could do with cars was amazing.

He had confided in me that he had never known his real father. His only reminder of him was a ring he wore that looked like a birthstone. I knew this ring was dear to George, and when he passed it to me in history class, I fingered the odd stone with feelings of compassion before I passed it back. "Going steady" was not for me. I knew I couldn't get serious with anyone until I was ready, and that it would take years for me to be ready.

. . .

After searching for my younger brother Jack Junior, I found him on the porch shortly after sunrise that day. He preferred to be called Jack now. I never told him, but I had dubbed him "my sunshine" because he was the only sensible, positive, and happy person in my immediate family, and I loved him very much.

He had the same wide grin, but with even white teeth, a long thin nose, slightly more pronounced than mine, the same eyes, and blonde hair that never seemed to want to behave. Being eleven months younger than me, he was shorter.

A strong sense of reality, a clear mind, and a passion for work was a winning combination for him. He was a quiet man, but when he spoke, it meant something because his decisive words were followed by action.

This day he was signing up for the United States Army, and I wanted to present him with my going-away present, a Snorkel pen, and ask him to write. I wanted to sign up too, but women had to wait until they were eighteen. I was stuck in Rhode Island for another year. He accepted the pen with that winning, knowing smile of his. The little rascal had big dreams that he hadn't shared with anyone, but before long, word that he was a member of the 101st Air Borne Division reached home. My brother was a parachutist.

. . .

Because the lure for adventure had long beckoned me too, like my brother, I aimed for the sky. As soon as I graduated from high school, I took the bus to the recruiting station in Pawtucket and was disappointed when they told me to come back when I turned eighteen. That was a month away. The criteria for enlistment were a high school education, passing two written tests, and tough physical examination. I also had to face the acute scrutiny of a psychiatrist. None of the examinations were difficult for me, but when I took the oath with twelve other girls, my stomach had a queasy feeling in it.

I was now a WAF, a woman in the air force. Our date of departure for Lackland Air Force Base in San Antonio, Texas, was September 27, 1954. Leaving home was more difficult than I had imagined it would be. I gave Mom and Granny a long hug, feeling the first traces of homesickness already, and left them on the walk in front of the old house, the place I felt was home, not daring to look back, lest I burst into tears. Uncle Jeffrey and Aunt Sherry took me to the airport in his junky Oldsmobile, and Dad, Lu, and the kids followed. Dad drove an old blue Cadillac, which was always full of tools.

We took an Eastern Air Lines Super Constellation from Hillsgrove Airport at 9:40 p.m. and flew to Washington, DC, where we picked up some new recruits. From there, we flew to San Antonio. It was a trip into the unknown for me, both filled with excitement and trepidation. And after I took one last look at the white tops of the capital buildings, the airplane began to tilt and rock back and forth, up and down.

Flying was not as romantic as I had imagined it to be. I had had visions of peering out of cockpits and whizzing by the ground at high speed. Now all I saw were clouds, and all I heard were gagging passengers. Stewardesses scurried around, carrying wet cloths and vomit bags, murmuring among themselves that it was the worst turbulence they had ever experienced.

I found myself wedged between two sick passengers and begged to be moved because the stench was getting to me. An attendant found mercy and moved me to the rear of the airplane with another recruit who also had a strong stomach. My newfound traveling companion, Olga, and I had a chance to chat, and because the seat was perpendicular to the other crowded rows of seats, I was able to look out at the blackness of the night sky and see an occasional deluge of water explode onto the window. How in the world the pilot was able to find his way through the dark storm was beyond me.

We landed in Houston, Texas, after a grueling night of wild weather. The sky was now a damp overcast. Stewardesses led us off the plane for a few minutes, the cabin was cleaned and the plane refueled. I was happy to breathe genuine air again even though the air outside was foul because of the smell of human excrement. Then we headed for Lackland. We landed there at 8:35 a.m. on the 28th.

The wide expanse of land surrounding the base made me feel empty inside. How could people live without trees, bushes, or flowers? I had a sinking feeling inside me as I stepped off the aircraft. The buildings on the base were flat and colorless. A few shrubs scattered here and there tried but failed to create the impression of home.

It was ninety degrees outside, and I was wearing a navy blue woolen suit and heavy tan coat with a high collar. The blue suitcases with the white leather trim that I so eagerly unwrapped at Christmas now were too heavy. They must've weighed a total of sixteen pounds empty, and with all the paraphernalia I had in them, my arms were strained to the point where they ached.

We walked in single file for what seemed like miles across the runway in the intense heat, and I was sure every step of the way that I wouldn't make it. Although my stomach had been kind to me on the flight, it now revolted in anger, and my knees followed suit by turning to mush.

I dragged my coat to lessen the load. The first impression I had tried to make now seemed unimportant. Then we sat for two hours in a non-ventilated room and stared at each other in silence because a sergeant with a face like a camel gave us strict orders not to talk and dared us to use the soda, candy bar, and gum machines that lined two sides of the room.

Finally, a gray bus arrived and took us to our squadron, where we were shuffled into what looked like a classroom of sorts to receive our pep talk.

"You do not belong to yourselves anymore. The air force owns you. You must obey orders without question. If you go AWOL (absent without leave), you could be put in prison, even shot."

It went on to describe in detail how much we owed our country for all it had done for us, our parents, our grandparents, and everyone else in the world. I don't know what the other girls were thinking, but I do know that the speech was enough to frighten one eighteen-year-old girl from Massachusetts to death, especially when someone told us that a girl had been run over by a car when she had jumped the barbed wire fence that surrounded the base. She had gone AWOL.

I had thought the worse was over after that horrid trip across country. But it was just beginning. The barracks were old bachelor officers' quarters (BOQs) that looked immaculate when we dragged our gear, including newly issued uniforms, bedding, and a heavy trench coat into the dayroom. Then we marched to the chow hall where we grabbed a tray and stood in another line while odors of hot coffee brewing, bacon, ham, eggs, and toast reached my nostrils, causing hunger pangs. Orange juice was never plentiful in my childhood home, but when my turn came, I grabbed three tall glassfuls, which tasted like nectar and devoured the food that was placed on my tray.

Outside of the food, the next few weeks of basic training was frustrating—to me at least. That first night, I slept between two cots because two recruits had rushed to the cots before I could get there, almost knocking me down. I found myself on the floor most of the night and cried myself to sleep each time I was awakened from the jolt of hitting the hard oak.

To my amazement, the barracks were not as immaculate as I had supposed. There was dirt in the corners that the tactical instructor (or TI) pointed out that I could reach with an old toothbrush (my old toothbrush because on our first payday, the TI presented us with a list of things we had to buy, which included a new brush for our teeth). That shine I had admired on the floors was not shine at all because we couldn't see the reflection of our faces in it.

It was a typical BOQ barracks with eight rooms and a latrine on each side and a large room in the center called the dayroom, where we gathered for meetings.

Cleaning and scrubbing, discipline, and marching became a way of life. Everyone was on edge. Our TI was known to us only as Airman Bruce. No one had a first name. Although it was stressful and tough for all of us, we were getting better acquainted in the process.

My best friends at Lackland were Ruth Latheid and a Southern belle we called Mississippi. Once, Ruth and I got into a tussle. She started it when she pulled my pillow off my bed. I took her pillow off. Then she undid my well-made bunk. I threw her blankets on the floor. We ended up in the middle of the dayroom, having a wrestling match. The other girls finally separated us.

After that, several of the girls began to "short-sheet" each other. It was fun. To short-sheet, one had to fold the bottom sheet in two vertically and remake the bed so that the person couldn't detect it. When she tried to get into bed at night she would be unable to stretch out her legs. Ruth and I short-sheeted "Mississippi's" bed.

I was surprised that I fared better than most of the other girls, including two of my roommates who broke down and cried the day before the white glove inspection. The white glove inspection was the most important event in basic training because it was used as a means of proving how well we could perform under stress.

We didn't know that, of course. All we knew was that a major so-in-so (I still don't remember her name) was coming to our barracks wearing white gloves, and that she would run those white gloves over and around and under everything, and if they should get dirty, we may "wash out" of basic training. Washing out of basic training would have meant that we would have to go home in absolute and utter disgrace. Along with being the cleanest, neatest people in the world, we had to stand at attention by our bunks and answer questions pertaining to the air force.

Where my strength came from I don't know, but I remained calm and collected and took charge of the situation by giving chores to the two girls. One of them, Pat Larkin, had been uppity up to this point, even treating me with disdain at times by ignoring me whenever I spoke to her.

Now she hid her face in her hands and repeated over and over, "I can't do it. I can't do it."

Pat Kittel, the other roommate and debutante of the bunch, cried openly and unashamedly.

Deah V. Kidd, the oldest roommate, whom I previously referred to as Captain Kidd because she constantly bossed the rest of us around, stood by me, offered suggestions, and assisted me in waxing and buffing under and inside the drawers, the outside and inside of cabinets, and just about everything in the room.

The big day finally came, We stood at attention by our bunks to wait for the major. My mind was in a whirl. Suppose she should ask me something I hadn't studied? We could hear her going from room to room and waited with bated breath until she came to ours.

She was a very attractive woman who never smiled, and her tailored uniform fit precisely. Her hands glided over our bunks to determine if the army blankets were stretched taut. Then she slid her hand over the bottom of one of the closets and checked our shoes to see if they were highly polished. She scrutinized each of us with her eyes and began to throw the questions at us. When she came to me, she asked, "What is the insignia of a major?"

I was in luck. We had been taught to stand erect with the heels of our shoes together, our toes slightly apart, our hands at our sides with the thumbs even with the seams on our skirts, and our eyes straight ahead. This I was doing, of course, and out of the corner of my left eye, I could clearly see a golden oak leaf on her shoulder.

"A gold oak leaf," I snapped.

She grabbed the front of my jacket and give it a tug.

"Good fit."

Little did she know that the pajamas under my uniform had filled in the wrinkles because I had no place else to hide them. We had only been allowed three dirty items in our laundry bag, and I already had stuffed a pair of fatigues and a pair of socks in there. Socks counted for two. It had worked out just fine because the air force had issued me a uniform that would've fit a girl fifteen pounds heavier.

The inspection lasted only forty-five minutes, but it seemed like hours. Then our TI called us into the dayroom to give us the results. She took a deep breath and looked sternly at each of us. The tension in the room was heavy. Then she smiled with a twinkle in her eyes, unable to hold back any longer.

"We have been awarded the distinguished title of 'honor barracks,' which means we are the cleanest WAF barracks on the entire base."

Shouts of "Whoopee!" and "Hurrah!" and sighs of relief filled the room, and we began to hug each other and cry for joy. Then we burst into laughter when word was passed along that one of the girls couldn't remember her name when the major asked her. Her name was Mary Smith.

We held the distinction of honor barracks until graduation from basic training in December of 1954. After receiving our first stripe, we returned to the barracks to pick up our assignments. Some of us were assigned as a group, others were not. Most went to work in the supply department. We were sent to all areas of the country.

My orders read ECM, and no one knew what that meant except Captain Kidd, who had been hoping to be assigned to electronics countermeasures herself. I was still bewildered as to why they had chosen me. After all, I had no college degree like dear Kidd and had graduated from high school with only a B minus average. But I did know that I was headed for Keesler Air Force Base in Biloxi, Mississippi, after a short leave to visit my family.

The cheerless day of departure brought tears to my eyes when I had to say goodbye to my newfound friends, and I wondered if there would be other friends who were as dear to my heart in other places and boarded a train that took me home for the holidays. I also took with me a feeling of accomplishment that was to stay with me for the rest of my life and eagerly looked forward to a bright and challenging future.

CHAPTER 5

The train chugged from Providence. Through Connecticut and New Jersey, through slums strewn with papers and garbage in New York City and Philadelphia, the scrubbed and shiny steps in front of the houses in Baltimore, through the spectacular hills of Virginia, through North Carolina, then South Carolina and Georgia and on to Alabama and Mississippi, where an unending series of bridges crossed us over marshlands and swamps until the Gulf of Mexico came into view.

I grabbed my luggage with excitement and anticipation when the conductor cried out the name of my destination. The sight of trees and an ocean brought fond memories to me, and even though the air was damp and muggy, my starched uniform scraped against my thighs when I climbed the steps of the bus which took me to the barracks, where an uproar greeted me as I opened the door. Girls were cheering, shouting, hugging, and squealing, and suitcases were piled topsy-turvy in the hall.

"A WAF's paradise! They say this is a WAF's paradise—a place where romance is sure to blossom," they yelled in unison. "New Orleans is only seventy-two miles away, and the atmosphere there is supposed to be gay and merry, unlike anywhere else in the entire world."

Amid the introductions and chattering, I overheard that Deah V. Kidd had been seen waterskiing in Florida, having the time of her life. I chimed in as soon as there was an opening, eager to learn all I could about the base and the school.

The Captain in charge of the 35th air training squadron at Keesler was Captain Clarice Masson. Cleaning was not a top priority. School was. All but three of us were taking a six-week training course learning how to transmit and receive Morse code. Phyllis Molotchick, Georgia L. Gibson, and I were assigned to eight months of comprehensive training in electronics. We were obliged to attend classes for five days a week, six hours a day.

The days began early. Roll call was at four, and after a five o'clock breakfast, we marched to school. When the sun reached its zenith in the sky, we were relaxing at the pool or eating in the cafeteria.

During the first three days of school, my mind felt like it was in the middle of a blizzard. I could not make sense of the barrage of facts that were being thrown at me. On the fourth day, I found myself in front of the adjutant's desk confiding in her my feelings of discouragement. Her advice was simple: "Just let your mind take in the information and relax. You probably understand more than you realize."

She was right. Ohms Law, capacitors, resistors, circuits, time constants, wave guides, and power supplies soon began to make sense to me, and I was tossing questions at the instructor that the rest of the class appreciated because they had difficulty understanding the material too.

The rumors were correct after all because almost every girl at Keesler in our barracks met the man of her dreams there. Two marriages took place also, although one was annulled and the second ended in divorce.

Romance came to me at Keesler too with all the intensity and excellence that poets have described from the beginning of time, even though it was platonic, to me at least. It was the first time I had fallen in love, although I didn't realize it at the time. Duane Harless and I walked on the beaches, kissed under the stars, celebrated in New Orleans, and shared our inner feelings, dreams, and ambitions.

We both knew that it was meant to be only for a brief moment in time because we each had plans for a future that didn't include the other, and that made it even sweeter and more special—sweet because it was innocent and special because I had never felt that way before.

On the day he flew off for Paris, France, he sent a friend to my school during recess to tell me he was leaving, and my soul was full of longing for him, even though I believed that there would be plenty of other men in my life at that time. I was wrong in a sense, though, because no one ever forgets that first love. I still think of him today whenever I see the sun set on a deserted beach.

Graduation was three weeks away for me too, and because "Gibby" and "Mo" had already been assigned to Keesler, I assumed that's where I would spend the rest of my air force career. To my surprise, when I finally received my orders they read, "78th Field Maintenance Squadron, 78th Fighter Group, Hamilton Air Force Base, San Rafael, California."

When Mo and Gibby put me on the train in front of the small station in Biloxi that looked like a scene from a Christmas postcard, I heard Mo ask Gibby, "Do you think she'll make it?"

Gibby's response was "No."

It took me almost fifty years to understand the significance of that conversation. They needn't have concerned themselves, however, because God was with me all the way. In New Orleans, as I sat with my suitcases at the station, fearful that I might miss the announcement for the departure of my next train and admiring the architecture in the station, a tall, handsome, well-groomed young man approached me and engaged me in conversation. To my relief I discovered that we were both headed for Los Angeles.

My self-appointed guide escorted me across the country, carried my luggage, treated me to excellent dinners in the dining car, identified all the places we passed by, and described in detail how the Rocky Mountains would appear out of nowhere, seeming to emerge out of the desert. He talked endlessly about his beloved

California, showed me photographs of his sports car, his lovely home, and his family. I could see no ill-intent in him. He was a real, honest-to-goodness, sincere, and wonderful person.

We traveled at night on the Sunset Route aboard the Southern Pacific Railroad on August 27 through the flatlands in Texas, New Mexico, and boundless desert in Arizona. In the dining car, our waiters poured coffee from exquisitely carved silver pots that were set on spotless linen tablecloths. Every meal was delightfully arranged on heavy silver dishes.

In the Arizona moonlight, the scattered cacti looked like monsters that flashed across the window. Yet the desert was serene in its own way. Velvet skies vanished suddenly when the orange mountains jumped at us from nowhere at dawn as my "guide" had told me. The awesome sight made me catch my breath.

After hours in the desert, traveling across California to Los Angeles seemed like minutes. Los Angeles lay sprawled across the hills; the houses were flat, usually made of stucco with orange serrated roofs and verandahs extended on the sides. My guide invited me to stay with his family for a spell, but my days of leave were limited, and I feared I would not make it to San Francisco in time.

The train arrived late, and I needed to transfer my ticket. My escort purchased the ticket, grabbed my luggage, and saw me on the northward-bound train called the Starlight. He asked me to stop and visit him if I ever came to Los Angeles again. I never expected that to happen, and it never did.

From the windows of the Starlight, I saw the calm waters of the Pacific pass by to my left and the orange crags of the Rocky Mountains on my right, on which the dwellings clung to the sides of the hills. California intrigued me, and I knew I wanted to spend as much time there as I could. In the evening I reached Hamilton, a quaint little base that nestled on the slopes of inclined hills near San Rafael.

Had I worked in electronics at Hamilton Air Force Base, I would have missed the biggest adventure of my lifetime. But the only ECM squadron on the base had no accommodations for women, so they shuffled me around from one job to another, not knowing quite what to do with me. First I worked in a radar shop with a technician in the 78ᵗʰ Fighter Group's field maintenance squadron. It was obvious that he didn't give a hoot whether I learned anything or not.

Undaunted, I swindled some radar repair manuals from the shelves and studied them until I felt I could take a test that would lead to a promotion. Then I got permission to see the commander to inquire about being tested to obtain a proficiency in electronics. My discussion with him led to frustration and anger. There was no way I could work in electronics. After the repair shop, they sent me to the production control office, where I was told that job was related to electronics, and if I tried hard I could possibly receive a promotion.

The air force lied to me again because three months later they sent me to work for the secretary of the captain in charge of the squadron. That did it. I had had enough. One day I went on strike. Instead of doing my job, I sat at my desk in front of an old Underwood typewriter with my arms folded across my chest and refused to work. My job was in electronics, not typing. It didn't matter what they did to me. I didn't care. Throw me in the brig. Take the second stripe I had worked so hard for. I earned that stripe, but you can have it. Take both my stripes. Kick me out of the air force. Good riddance.

I had expected to lose my career, or worse, but it didn't matter to me at that point. Inez Belotti, the secretary, was kind enough to lend a sympathetic ear to my complaints even though her desk was piled high with work, and I was not offering to help her with it.

She had complete confidence in Captain Schultz, our commander, and told him of my dilemma. Captain Schultz, a tall, thin, craggy-looking man, rubbed a weather-beaten hand across his chin, scowled, and said nothing. At Inez's request, he looked for an opening in air force regulations that would bring about a solution to my problem. Inez convinced me not to worry.

Realizing that someone was listening to my grievances at long last, I relaxed. In the weeks that followed Inez, Captain Schultz, and Tech Sergeant Sprecker, the liaison sergeant, and I became good buddies.

One day, while I was busy typing, a general came into the office and asked for the captain.

"Oh, he's not in, sir," I said absently, hardly looking up from my typewriter.

"Young lady, don't you know that it's customary to stand at attention when a general comes into a room?"

I snapped to attention and shouted, "Yes, sir."

He went into the office for a few minutes, and when he returned, I jumped up again.

"Only the first time, airman, only the first time," he said as he strode past.

That first encounter with a general made me a bit apprehensive, and as I was sorting out the pile that was on Inez's desk one day, I decided to type out a poem about generals for Captain Schultz. He laughed so loud when Inez showed it to him I could hear him in the front office. Then he hung it on a wall for the general to see. The general chuckled when he read the poem, and after that he would chortle whenever he marched by me. Because work with Inez and Captain Schultz was cheerful, I almost forgot about my plight.

One day, Captain Schultz approached me. "Airman Midsummer, there's a position available for flight attendant I would like you to apply for. If you are interested, I think you can transfer your specialty code in electronics over to air traffic control. Would you like to become a flight attendant?"

Was I interested? Do birds like to fly? A chance to work on an aircraft and fly to places that I had only dreamed about? To be able to socialize with the crew and the passengers? He must be kidding. It can't be true.

The possibility became a reality after three months of paper work, negotiations, and several interviews. At one point I was denied after an interview with a psychiatrist when I stated, "The air force is driving me nuts."

I contested that outlandish report from the psychiatrist that made me appear to be unstable when it came back from

Washington, DC. Even though that unfortunate circumstance postponed my application, my request was eventually approved.

Before I left Hamilton, my friend Arvena Pearl Scott or "Scotty" as we called her, held a party in my honor at the NCO club. All my friends, Lois, Beck (her fiancé), Sherry, Rosie Smith, Betty Kirk, Jeanette Graves, Donna Williams, Mary Marvelle, Barbara Nash, "Cuz" (our barracks sergeant whose bed Scotty and I put a block of ice in), and all their boyfriends gave me a warm sendoff.

Two days later, Lois and Truet Beck drove me to the ferry. Across the bay, I boarded the California Zephyr on the Redwood Empire Route of the Northwest Pacific that took me to Denver, Colorado, on July 23, 1956. I was thrilled that I had taken the vista dome, which had enabled me to see more of the Rockies.

In Denver, I stayed overnight in the YWCA and boarded the Southern Pacific in the morning. This time I was traveling through the central part of our country where I hit a part of Kansas, Missouri, Tennessee, and Georgia. Wheat fields in Kansas stretched for miles. My destination was Palm Beach Air Force Base in West Palm Beach, Florida.

Just outside of Alabama, word was passed along to me that another WAF was on board, and I checked every car on the train from the back of the engine to the caboose, until I spotted another uniform crowded in a corner hemmed-in by other passengers. The air force dress blues were being worn by Leller Wisdom, a quiet unassuming airman first class who was two years my senior. Angel hailed from Oregon, and her speech and manner convinced me that she was intelligent, and I liked her immediately. We were both looking forward to our six weeks of flight attendant school together.

Palm trees, highway number 1, and railroad tracks which ran parallel to each other heralded in the news that we were traveling down the Atlantic coast in Florida. A warm but gentle breeze made the hot, humid air bearable when we jumped off the train. The base itself looked dull and colorless. I had expected more of Florida because it had always been a tourist state, but only the palm trees delighted me during my stay there.

Schooling there was similar to that at Keesler. We arose early, attended class for six hours a day, and dove into the pools every afternoon. On one occasion, we were able to swim in the Atlantic, and I could not discern much difference between those highly publicized shores and the ones at home.

While stationed at West Palm Beach, I became painfully aware of my shortcomings. In basic training I had been a star; in electronics I shone. I was surrounded by attractive, talented, intelligent, and competent girls, all with better qualities than I had.

In class, I merely got by. I not only was no one's favorite, but I also didn't seem to mix in well with the rest of the airmen. Nevertheless, Angel and I became and remained the best of friends.

Upon graduation, I took a well-needed thirty-five-day leave of absence, climbed aboard an Eastern Air Lines Zephyr and headed for home so I could rest and get coddled. My feelings of inferiority were tossed aside when I returned to the accolades. Mom doted on me, my father, Aunt Sherry, and Uncle Jeffrey were so proud of me they beamed from ear to ear. Sam was still in the hospital, Marla was in high school, and Jack Junior was in France. Eventually, though, I was anxious to return to work.

Determined to see as much of our fabulous country as I possibly could, I decided to use part of my extended leave by taking the Greyhound to California, where I was to be stationed next. From Providence to Boston, familiar territory blinked at me from the windows of the bus, but when the nose of the large vehicle pointed westward toward Chicago, I strained my eyes in order to take in what was for me uncharted waters. The cities and towns were similar to those in New England.

Outside of Chicago, when we stopped in Niles, Michigan, for a coffee break, the bus driver suggested that I not stay overnight in the big city because as he put it, "A young girl alone would not be safe in that town." I heeded his warning, registered in the Four Flags Hotel in Niles, the place he recommended, took a well-needed steaming hot bath in a cute little old-fashioned tub, dressed in a fresh uniform, and took him up on his offer for dinner.

When I sat across from him in the small restaurant and he removed his cap, I realized he was much older than I had imagined. He was almost completely bald. I also had an uneasy feeling that he may have had ulterior motives and felt very immature and frightened.

My fears were ungrounded, however, because even though he may have had those kinds of ideas at first, he treated me in the same manner that one would treat his younger sister. His words of caution and concern stayed with me and encouraged me for the rest of my journey.

The next day I hopped on a bus that would take me to the big bad city. When I arrived it was evening, and I hiked across a bridge near the terminal to view the lights of the metropolis. There were cars and train tracks, crossing and zigzagging this way and that, and gigantic buildings that were breathtaking.

Lights twinkled on and off like stars, as the city life hustled and bustled around me. I refused a date with a cab driver who asked me to stay overnight in the city so he could take me around to show me the sights because this time I dared not take anyone up on any invitation.

From Chicago I took the bus through more wheat fields in Iowa where countless miles of upright bales of wheat stood at attention as we passed. The flat acreage of Nebraska greeted us next. We made a short stop in Omaha, then headed north to Rapid City, South Dakota, and the Badlands.

I never could understand why they called them the "badlands" because the black mountains looked inviting to my weary, bloodshot eyes. I slept soundly that night after a hot shower, and hailed a cab the next morning for a sightseeing tour of the black hills. The taxicab driver in South Dakota, who was jolly and good-natured, took me to lunch during the tour and snapped a photograph of me in front of the Rushmore Monument. I also took photos of the dinosaurs.

Later that afternoon, I grabbed the bus again and headed for "the mile-high city" of Denver, Colorado, where the thin oxygen exhausted me. After resting at a small hotel in town, I braced myself for the rugged terrain that would take us through Cheyenne, Wyoming, to Salt Lake City, where I expected to look up Mo's parents.

The beautiful city of Salt Lake with its surrounding gray mountains was by far the most impressive and loveliest chapter in my cross-country trek so far. No wonder Brigham Young and his followers, the Mormon, believed they had reached the Promised Land when they came across this Mecca in the middle of the desert!

After reserving a room at the Hotel Temple Square, I refreshed, scanned the telephone book for their address, grabbed a small trinket at the hotel gift shop, and showed up unannounced at Mo's mother's apartment. I could see Mo's resemblance in her mother's surprised face and felt that she was disappointed when I informed her that I was only planning to pay her a short visit, but I was not one to impose. Instead I took in the sights of the city on my own, which included the Mormon Brigham Young and the Mormon Pioneers monuments and the Mormon Temple and was on my way again.

We made a brief stop in Reno, Nevada in the middle of the night, where I lost two quarters to a "one-armed bandit." My money had always been scarce, and I resented the gall of this lifeless machine with all the bright colors that took my money away. I was definitely not gambler material.

By the time I reached San Francisco, my left eye was completely closed from exhaustion, and my body was racked with pain caused by fatigue. Because I wanted to arrive in San Rafael fully rested, I checked in at the Golden Gate Hotel, soaked in a hot tub, donned a charcoal suit I had reserved for the last leg of my journey, and ventured downstairs to the Golden Bubble lounge for a glass of ginger ale and to hear Frank O'Keefe tinkle on the piano keys.

My repose was interrupted by a gentleman who tried to pick me up, but the bartender shooed him away. Returning to my room, I slept soundly for sixteen hours. When I awoke I could open my eye, but even today this eye twitches when I am overtired.

Early the next morning, I rode the bus up Highway 101 to Hamilton Air Force Base, where Scotty and Lois extended a warm welcome to me. It was good to be back again, if only for a couple of days.

My final destination still lay ahead, and the sight of it when I finally did arrive caused my body to tense. It had taken me nine days to snake my way across America.

Travis Air Force Base, a strategic air command (or SAK for short), which meant that it housed long-range bombers and fighters, also contained an air transport squadron, of which I was to be a part. Its runways, hangars, and gray buildings stretched across Sacramento, California, like a flood that had taken over the adjacent countryside and engulfed its cities and towns. This, for better or worse, was where I had pledged to spend the rest of my enlistment.

CHAPTER 6

"Hello. My name is Ruth Midsummer. Welcome aboard MATS flight 237 from Sacramento, California, to Honolulu, Hawaii," I would announce over the loud speaker, relishing every moment of it.

Being the center of attention was grand. I enjoyed giving the predeparture and pre-landing speeches so much that many of my fellow flight attendants requested that I do them for them. I adlibbed and put the passengers at ease with my humor.

That wasn't the only excitement that flying brought to me that I loved . . . I often convinced the aircraft commander into allowing me to sit in the "jump seat," which was located diagonally behind and to the left of his seat when he was flying the aircraft, so I could watch him land the plane. This was only possible to achieve on landings to Wake Island.

From that vantage point I could see the tiny, seven-mile island appear larger and larger until its single runway was directly beneath us. I heard the signals the pilot gave to the copilot, saw him maneuver the wheel, and felt the thump of the landing gear as it came in contact with the pavement. My heart would thump in unison.

On one occasion, during a flight to Wake where we carried only cargo, Captain Crystal allowed me to sit in the copilot's seat and take over the controls. He taught me how to maneuver a turn, which I was able to complete myself.

Our normal route was from Travis Air Force Base to Hawaii, to Wake Island and then to Tokyo, Japan, where we would pick up another aircraft and head back by the same path. We usually were allowed a twelve-hour crew rest on every leg of the journey, except Tokyo, where we enjoyed twenty-four hours of free time. There were exceptions, of course. When we experienced engine trouble, the rest period could last for days.

All in all, I landed in Hawaii approximately eighty times and the rest of the places half that much, earning my wings after 250 hours of air time.

Being in Tokyo was like being in another world, with the Ginza markets that lined the city streets, its rickshaws, tiny houses, massage parlors, and strange nightspots that were bordered on two sides with curtains rather than walls. The toilet bowls looked like spittoons from an old Western movie.

Everything about the Japanese people fascinated me, especially their art. Their small hands carved intricate figures on everything from jewelry to fabric, and I took home numerous souvenirs for myself and for my family. Japanese tailors fashioned three suits for me: a cashmere, a gray flannel, and a green gabardine. They also stitched an ankle-length gray camelhair coat for me. Shopping at the ginza market, an ancient version of our flea markets, became a passion for me.

I purchased lovely hand-painted jewelry boxes, one for Mom and one for me, chopsticks just for the heck of it, a Japanese robe called a "kimono," dresses, pottery, and many other extravagances. The Japanese people were great imitators. They imitated our music, our inventions, and our people. They seemed to want to copy everything American, which I thought was sad because they were a gifted people themselves.

But Wake Island was my favorite stop because I felt like it was my very own tropical island in the Pacific, which I shared with only my crew and the Philippine boys who worked there. The waters of the lagoon near "Lefty's Reef," a small saloon at the end of a pier that stuck out on the ocean, were warm. When I donned my scuba diving equipment, which was available at no charge to crewmembers, and dove into the blue waters, multicolored tropical fish glided over and under and beside me, above the sharp gray coral which sometimes cut my skin. My hair turned a golden yellow from the sun, which delighted me to no end.

We all enjoyed the succulent meals that were cooked to order and the steaks that were served on Wednesday and Saturday at the only chow hall.

Honolulu, Hawaii, was a disappointment to me, however, because I found it to be too commercialized, even though the crowded beaches were beautiful and there were some historical sites like Pearl Harbor on the island of Oahu that I would not have missed.

Back at Travis, Angel was my barracks sergeant and still my best friend. Dates were plentiful to all the WAFs, but I made certain that Angel and I double dated most of the time, since I was still trying to decide what falling in love was all about. I knew only one thing for certain: no man was ever going to treat me cruelly like Dad had treated Mom.

Most of the men I met in the service were respectful to me, however, and I received two marriage proposals while stationed at Travis. I, in turn, loved all the boys in my own way, even though not one of them ever got close to my sacred virginity. I had no idea then how a man made love to a woman, having never seen explicit movies nor read that type of literature, and I was not anxious to find out. I simply enjoyed being attracted to and having men be attracted to me and was in love with the whole idea of it.

I also had decided that if I didn't find the man of my dreams while I was in the air force, I would attend Bible college, become a missionary, and somehow make a difference in the lives of others. I had long wanted to end some of the suffering in this world, and if I never got the chance to do so, my life would not have been complete. Boys definitely were in second place.

My career was on an upward climb as well. One day, when I was having lunch in Hawaii with Captain Wilson, per his request, in general conversation I mentioned some suggestions I had that would improve my job as flight attendant. I thought nothing of this conversation with my aircraft commander, until I found myself in front of the promotion board four weeks later.

They requested that I submit my ideas in writing. I did, and I received the only stripe that was awarded to the WAF squadron at that time. They had chosen me out of a hundred girls. My mother was thrilled to receive a letter from the air force informing her that she should be proud to have a daughter like me. I was flying high in more ways than one. And when one is flying too high, one is apt to crash.

One of the girls in my squadron, Leota Wilson, and I had been competing for flights because the squadron commander insisted that we take turns rotating our work in the orderly room and on flights. One day, I managed to be assigned to a flight by begging permission of our flight sergeant. And acting like a smart aleck, I dared to peek into the orderly room and brag about it to Sergeant Prince, our first sergeant. I was returning from my pre-flight briefing with the crew and believed that it was safe to boast about it.

Now Sergeant Prince was a cruel and crafty man. Every one of us in the orderly room had witnessed him belittle Tech Sergeant Markus, his junior non-commissioned officer, many times, in a variety of vicious ways, both verbally and physically. He sometimes would yank the chair out from under Markus as he was about to sit down, or steal objects from his desk, and when Markus would search for them, he would laugh that cruel laughter of his. He did all this knowing full well that Sergeant Markus was too timid to fight back because he feared he would be dishonorably discharged for attacking a superior.

Also, when Sergeant Prince wasn't committing these unkind acts, he would refer to his second in command as a wino because of his drinking habit. Sergeant Markus had seen too much action on the frontlines and was clinging to his job desperately until he was able to retire. Retirement was still two years away.

Because I dared to confront this bully, he pulled me off the flight and sent Leota instead. I was furious. My anger came to an abrupt end when, three days later, word that the aircraft Leota and the rest of the seven-man crew and fifty-seven passengers was missing reached our ears. The last report that came from the radio operator was they were two hundred miles outside of Tokyo, and all was well.

My first reaction was shock, accompanied by disbelief and feelings of horror. Guilt then took over. It should have been me, not Leota. She was the neat one, the smart one. She should have received that stripe, not I. Although I welcomed danger myself because I found it to be exhilarating, to have someone else go to an icy grave in the Pacific in my place was another matter.

Our commander sent all of us on flights as soon as possible. Some of our aircraft searched for wreckage. The air force called in air, sea, and rescue operations. The navy sent ships to the area. Japanese ships searched the Pacific waters near Tokyo. And we called our folks, assuring them that we were all fine. No life raft, no piece of wreckage, no human remains were ever found.

What remained for me was the beginning of tremors and fear. The monster was regaining its hold on me, and this time it never released me from its grasp. One day, soon after the crash, as I was making out the lunch list for the crew members as was customary, my hands began to tremble. Even though I had always had unsteady hands, this time it embarrassed me so much that I developed a fear, or a phobia, of writing in public. If anyone happened to be watching me write, the fear was loosed.

I developed a fear of the fear, or a second fear. I was afraid a situation might arise in which my fear would be manifested. The fear would begin hours ahead of time. At first I tried to get it out of my mind. If I denied it to myself or tried to ignore it, maybe it wouldn't happen.

The inevitable always came to pass, however. The time of dread came without fail, and it came with a power and a force so strong that it was too much for me to handle. I could not deny it then, could not avoid it. All I could do was suffer.

I would be standing in front of the counter, pen in hand, and then my hand would begin to tremble—slowly at first. My pulse would quicken. My heart would begin to beat at an alarming rate. Soon my hand would shake spasmodically. Then the rest of my body would follow suit—convulsing all over. I would hang on tightly to the pen, forcing it to write, take a deep breath, and bite my tongue. Nothing helped.

Someone will notice, I panicked. Someone will be able to tell by the chicken scrawls. Someone will find out, and I'll be so ashamed.

Then something else happened that made matters worse. I transferred my fear over to my dates. Whenever I sat across from a boy I was attracted to, my hands would tremble. That caused me no end of grief because most of the guys I dated invited me out to dinner. My career was in jeopardy, and my personal life was threatened.

Since I couldn't beat this thing, I had to devise other means of dealing with it. I became skillful in covering up and developed methods of avoiding a situation where my hands might vibrate. When I was scheduled for flights, I would bargain with another flight attendant, exchanging duties with him/her, like putting on the headrest or doing the briefings in return.

On dates, I would insist on sitting beside my boyfriend rather than across the table from him. Or I would suggest eating out in dimly lit places where my hands wouldn't easily be seen. That wasn't always possible though, depending on the situation.

Usually, fearful and miserable, I had to tolerate the shame and humiliation of twitches that were becoming more and more uncontrollable. I could not eat at all on dates, could not perform my duties as a flight attendant.

I was very much ashamed of this secret which I shared with no one, not with Lee, and not with my Aunt Sherry. The thought of getting help for my problem never, ever occurred to me. I suffered in silence, and it played havoc with the rest of my life.

I didn't realize nor guessed then that I suffered from a phobia, anxiety, and the onset of manic-depression, a disease which usually materializes in the early twenties. And I still did not associate my mental problems with those of my brother. I was an isolated case, I thought. No one else in the entire world was like me.

I did my best to be happy in spite of my problem, which loomed over me most of the time like a dark cloud, menacing and threatening to cause me harm. And way down deep inside me, I knew not where, I realized something terrible was going to happen to me someday because of it.

I live with it all by myself, and I even hoped beyond hope at times that it was a figment of my imagination. None of my friends ever suspected that I was anything but a fully confident human being. No one guessed. No one knew.

CHAPTER 7

I retired from the United States Air Force on September 26, 1957, and spent seven months in San Francisco with Scotty and other friends. During that time, I saw more of California and met some terrific people. Then I headed for home. This time I took the northern route on the Western Star aboard the Great Northern Railway, which took me through Oregon, Washington State, through the northern part of Idaho, Montana, North Dakota, to Wisconsin, on down to Chicago.

I was awed by the beauty of the snow-laden mountains of Glacier National Park in Montana which I viewed through the vista dome on top of the coach. By the time I reached Rhode Island, I had been in at least a bit of every one of these United States, except Alaska, which wasn't a state at that time.

Determined to somehow help every one of my suffering family members in some way by sharing with them all the knowledge I had managed to stuff in my head, I came home a happier and more optimistic person than I had ever been. Life had been good to me since I had left home for the most part, and I was hoping that this "thing" that I had in my head would go away in time if I could only keep putting it on the back burner of my mind.

My brother Jack Junior and I were two returning heroes. When we met for the first time in four years, he was thrilled that he was now a whole half inch taller than I was. Mom was happy to have her two travelers home with her, and Auntie Sherry and Uncle Jeffrey doted on me. My baby sister was still shy and remained distant from boys, but she too welcomed me joyously.

We soon settled down to routine, and I discovered that my younger brother was in love. I was very happy for him. I was slated for college in September and had enrolled in Gordon College in Massachusetts.

I went to visit my brother Samuel in the hospital with Mom one day, and I shall never forget that experience, even though it is so vague in my memory. I remember a dark, dreary corridor with young boys on either side. I think there were bars, or something that resembled bars, in front of them, and their arms were protruding through the bars.

When these young boys saw me, most of them averted my gaze and stared downward as if ashamed. I was dressed up that day in my Sunday best, having recently come from church services, and I felt guilty for looking so pretty. Sam was in the room at the end of the corridor, and I don't believe he recognized me at first. Then his eyes brightened a little.

He also must have thought that I didn't recognize him because he introduced himself as "the boy Sam who used to live with us." He then told me that they had tied him up and took him there in order for him to "cure" others. He told me that one man in the hospital had lost his finger, and that he had performed a miracle by replacing it for him. He even demonstrated how this was done by using his hands!

The entire experience was unnerving and horrible to me, so much so that I did not go with Mom the following Sunday. I wish I had. I was at home when the telephone rang. Mom's quivering, hysterical voice was on the other end of the line.

She told me that Sam's body was swollen when she first saw him, and she had left him the food she had brought and went to find his doctor. Before she could reach anyone, however, she heard a loud speaker bellow out Sam's name. That's when she called me.

I calmed her down as best as I could and assured her I would call my father in order to catch a ride to the hospital. After I hung up, I got down on my knees. I had long prayed for my brother's recovery, but now I was so overwhelmed by the tragedy of his suffering that I asked God to end it.

I don't know how long I stayed there, but while I was praying, I felt a comforting, peaceful feeling. It was as if a hand had reached way down deep inside me and took away the hurt. I knew then that my prayers had been answered. As I was still kneeling, the phone rang again, and Mom's wailing voice told me that Sam had died. I knew then he was with God.

Dad and I rushed to Mom's assistance. Tears of regret streamed down his face. His crying was so bad I don't know how he could have seen to drive. He had always blamed himself for Sam's illness.

When we arrived, we heard that Sam had choked to death on a piece of fruit Mom had brought for him. The irony of the whole situation was one more cruel spoke in the wheel of horror that Mom had to live through.

Doctors had tried desperately in the seven years he was confined to cure him. As is often the case, they try harder with the younger ones. They experimented with every type of medication that was at their disposal and worked very hard with all the psychological help that was available to them. Nothing seemed to work. He remained hopelessly psychotic.

Afterward, I helped my mother make the funeral arrangements. Because the coroner had ruled accidental death, Mom received double indemnity, which paid the entire cost of the funeral as long as we kept the expenses down. I had to persuade Mom to purchase the modestly priced casket, which was no mean task, because she wanted to spare no expense for the son she had nursed for so long.

Mom was in agony. At the wake, no one could comfort her. When Samuel was in his casket, a bug lit on him and she got very upset. She whisked the insect away, telling it to "wait until he was in the ground."

I cried more than anyone else did. Not that I felt the pain more. In fact, now that my brother's suffering was over, it felt like a great weight was lifted off my heart. Before then, I had been unable to shed tears for a long time. Now all my pent-up emotions were released. It was like a dam inside me had burst, and the river of tears came streaming forth unchecked. I cried for an entire week.

Many people had loved Sam. Friends we hadn't seen in years came to offer condolences. But there was no comfort for Mom. She kept asking over and over why God had taken her son, and no one could give her a satisfactory answer.

More tragedies were in store for her. Shortly after my brother's death, one of her legs began to fail her whenever she attempted to walk. The problem was caused by a cancerous tumor in her uterus. Doctors performed a hysterectomy.

While Mom was in the hospital, Granny was admitted as well. Granny's problem was colorectal cancer. Mom recovered but my grandmother was not as fortunate. The doctors gave her six months to a year to live. It took two years for this strong woman to succumb, two years in which she fought the disease, a battle that she eventually lost.

Mom had always been close to her mother, and she nursed her until the end. But the strain of caring for Granny, and the combination of the two deaths almost caused her to become ill again. She cried daily, telling everyone she was going to die, and was so convinced of her impending doom that no one wanted to stay there with her. She went around all day moaning that the doctors weren't telling her the truth, and that she was going to die like Samuel.

Her disease was all in her imagination, however, and it wasn't until her doctor wisely advised that she return to work that she began to see the truth. During all that time, no one noticed Marla because we all were preoccupied with our own problems. We were surprised when she sought psychiatric help and admitted herself into a detoxification center. There, she took the cure for drug addiction.

Later she told me that they had stripped off all her clothes and put her in a padded cell. She screamed and kicked until she was totally exhausted. Blood was coming out of her mouth from where she bit her tongue.

This "cold turkey" method was very cruel, especially to a shy twenty-one-year-old girl. No one had realized that her addiction to prescription drugs had gone this far. She apparently had been unable to sleep, and doctors had prescribed sleeping pills. For a while she was "cured."

When I was in the service, I had tried to make her stay in school so she could do something with her life. But she never had enough drive. Still, she had an innocent charm about her, and when Mom got her a job at Swanks Inc. in Attleboro, they made her the mail girl.

The owner's son took a liking to her and wanted to date her. But every time he started to speak to her, her face would turn beet red and she would retreat to the ladies' room.

Because of her inability to interact with people, it soon became apparent that she couldn't work for a living. She began taking days off work—at first a day here and there—and then for weeks at a time. Once, she missed work for two entire weeks, and she never called in to give the company an excuse or a reason for her absence. The personnel manager called her to ask her to return to work. She returned to work that time, but eventually, she never showed up for work at all.

I thought (as everyone else did) that she was lazy. And spoiled. Then her inactivity progressed until she didn't even want to get out of bed. Eventually, she couldn't sleep well at all. That led her to develop a fear of insomnia, and she frantically sought help from many angles.

We did not realize that these were signs that the dreadful fiend was grabbing onto her. In the '50s, a new class of wonder drugs were coming on the market, and some doctors may have been too anxious to prescribe them without fully checking on the patient's background.

That was the case with my sister. She enlisted the services of several physicians at once and took all kinds of pills to get to sleep.

She tried over-the-counter drugs as well. This mixing and matching of drugs eventually caused addiction.

Coinciding with it all was her quest for a steady job. That perhaps more than anything else shows her endless courage. She tried many jobs, from babysitting and office work, to being manager of a Cumberland Farms store. None of them lasted for more than three months.

She would try again and again. It was unbelievable, but she had an amazing ability to get jobs. She was, for a time, a waitress, a counter person at Dunkin' Donuts, a payroll clerk, and a clerk at city hall. Although she was no genius, she was fairly intelligent and had a pleasing personality. But she failed over and over to keep a job.

Jack Junior recognized this when he came home from his hitch in the army in June. He was always willing to help the family and had sent money for Mom to get her driver's license and an automobile so she could more easily visit Sam in the hospital. He also sent her money to obtain her former name back because that was the name her children carried. Mom had been hurt by unsuccessful marriages and had no wish to marry again.

Also, when he saw what was happening to Marla, he wanted to help. He now had a high-paying job in construction and could afford to spend some of it to make things better at home. He offered to give Mom enough money to take Marla to see a psychiatrist. He would have paid all the doctor bills.

Mom would not hear of such a thing because she was afraid that a doctor would admit Marla into a "crazy house," as she called it. Mom clung to Marla as much as Marla did to her. Theirs was a bond that transcended anyone's comprehension. No one could interfere.

She babied her daughter until she was totally emotionally crippled, without fully understanding what she was doing. In her mind, she was trying to prevent the illness that had ruined Samuel's life from happening to her daughter. She coddled, she waited on, and she put up with my sister's outbursts of violence and refused to get help for her. The rest of us could see what was happening, but it did no good.

. . .

As for me, Gordon College had been an absolute failure. My first (and last) night there, none of my three roommates showed up for various reasons. And the rest of the girls down the hall had some ideas about religion that were foreign to mine.

Wearing lipstick, listening to rock 'n roll music, hemlines that were in style (to the knees at that time), and cutting of the hair were all detestable sins to them. I knew that I could not adapt to their way of thinking and still remain honest to myself.

I stayed in my room and sobbed all through the night, and in the morning, I called my brother and asked him to take me back home. The next day, my minister found out my dilemma and enrolled me in Providence/Barrington Bible College in Rhode Island. He explained to me that I could commute to college, thereby enabling me to maintain my own views. I did this for a year.

I got myself an apartment, and because I knew it was unhealthy for my sister to live with Mom, I invited her to join me. She moved in with me, and I hoped to teach her to take care of herself. My schedule was very grueling. After going to classes, I worked every night in a department store until 10 p.m. and on Saturdays. Many nights I studied until 2 a.m.

I urged her to help me clean the apartment, to no avail. Even though I was exhausted on weekends, I did the grocery shopping, cleaned the apartment, and cooked. My sister paid no attention to my pleas for help, even when I taught her how to cook, and she returned home to the security of Mom and her bed.

I thought she was doing this by choice, never realizing that this was how the disease was working in her. What I believed was laziness was actually depression. That, coupled with low self-esteem, made her cling to her pillow, which had become a symbol of safety and security against the rest of the world.

But I blamed her and Mom. She was lazy, and Mom had made her that way by spoiling her. In my anger, I had condemned the both of them. I was the judge and the jury. Now I realize that others may misinterpret the actions of the mentally ill that way.

That year I lost twenty-five pounds from exhaustion and retired from school, even though I made the dean's list. I could see no future in studying the Bible and was disappointed with school because of the religious prejudice between Protestants and Catholics that was taught there.

But I did not give up on my sister. It was too late to help Sam, but it might not be too late for her. I thought that if she had a better social life, she might straighten out. Was I ever wrong!

My brother and a friend and I took her to a nightspot where she met an unscrupulous character named Seth Antonio. I confess that when I saw her dancing with him that night in her favorite lavender dress, I was envious because he was a handsome man. They went out a few times, then he took her out on New Year's Eve, and then he took her parking.

There, with only stars as witnesses, they made love. It was her first time. She had held her feelings in for many years, but now, believing she was in love, she couldn't control them. When it was over she burst into tears, which made him very angry. He began to rave and told her that she would end up in an institution. He also told her that he'd never marry her because she was not Catholic like he was. She was destroyed.

Even so, she was obsessed with him. For two years she frequented every nightclub that she thought he might go to. She found it impossible to believe that he couldn't care for her the way she cared for him. The whole episode changed her life for the worse. For the next seven years, she dated the drunks and the misfits in society.

I lived in the old homestead until Granny's death. I was satisfied that Granny went to heaven because I had witnessed to her before she died. Then Mom, Marla, and I moved into an apartment. I had managed to keep the monster at bay in my life so far. No one yet had guessed my secret. I had acquired a job with the Nay Department that was challenging and I decided to look for Mr. Right and settle down like other girls did.

Marla would sit down on the rocking chair all day and do nothing. She wouldn't even wash her own clothes or make her own meals. Mom did all that after work. It was becoming more and more intolerable for me to watch. I told Mom over and over to make her do something. I explained to her that it was unhealthy for Marla to do this. Mom refused to do anything. She simply couldn't see the harm she was doing.

The situation was becoming more and more intolerable for me. I had watched the horror show as long as I could, and I told Mom that, unless Marla did some work around the house, she was going to get sick, and I couldn't bear to watch it happen. I told her I would leave.

All my admonishing did no good, however, and I went to live with Auntie Sherry and Uncle Jeffrey in an attempt to forget all my difficulties. Again I sought escape. Again I thought of myself. After that, I saw Mom only when she phoned with her problems.

The following year I received an anxious call from my mother, informing me that Marla had overdosed on pills, and that she was taking her to the hospital. When I arrived, my sister was on a stretcher. I asked Marla whether or not she had taken pills and how many because I didn't trust her. She would not answer.

The attending nurse told her to strip. I shall never forget the anger that burned inside me that day because it built up to resentment toward my sister in the years that followed. The pity was gone now. Vanished. Through gritting teeth I insisted that my sister pay the hospital bill. They complied because my sister was of age.

That didn't end her attempts at suicide, however. For the next decade she tried to kill herself in a variety of ways, and in some cases she hurt herself badly. She downed at least three bottles of pills: cold remedies, aspirin tablets, and Aunt Sarah's prescription. She slashed her wrists on another occasion so badly that the scars are still noticeable.

She jumped from a second floor window and got a concussion. And perhaps the most dangerous thing she did was jump off a bridge onto a highway. She broke both ankles that time. I erroneously believed that if she really was serious about killing herself, she would have done so already. How wrong I was! Her cries for help were getting desperate, and her tortured mind was becoming worse.

CHAPTER 8

Moving in with my aunt and uncle seemed to be the course to follow. I loved them dearly. In fact, I had "adopted" them as my mother and father because they filled a void I had in my life. Having an intact family was something I had missed during my childhood.

My green and white Metropolitan was my new toy. With the tiny sports car I flew across the highway and zigzagged my way through traffic. Whenever there was a long line at a traffic light, I got there first by passing the cars on the right using the sidewalk.

Although the automobile was registered for only three passengers, I carried as many as ten people at a time. Sometimes I would drive the car around and around in a circle with my half sisters and my cousin Mitch in it to give the kids a thrill.

I wondered why I had this obsession with speed and where I got the energy from. It seemed that there was no end to it. I went out dancing to the tune of almost anything. Round and round I went, dancing the jitterbug to rock 'n roll music. I especially liked the Spanish dances: the rumbas, sambas, the tangos. I came alive when the melody of any kind burst forth. It seemed to satisfy a need I had deep within my being.

One night, while dancing at a nightclub, I met a tall, rugged man who looked like Duane Harless, my platonic love of long ago.

He fit the template that I had in my mind of the perfect man. I was convinced that I was in love again. But my feelings for him turned out to be disastrous for me. When I found out he was engaged to someone else, I decided that I would marry someone too. It didn't matter whether or not I was in love anymore.

That illusion had come to a dead end. The perfect opportunity presented itself in the person of one Rey Harvey. Rey was infatuated with me and kept begging me to marry him. At first I resisted, but gradually, he wore me down. Why not? He had enough love for both of us.

During my engagement with Rey, I often went out drinking with him at nightclubs, and on these occasions I engaged in petting with him. This closeness awakened sexual desires within me that had previously remained dormant. I am ashamed to say I let it go this far.

Although my virginity was still intact, my morals were tainted. Finally, on the day when we were to make arrangements for the wedding, I realized I could not go through with it. When I broke up with him, I hurt him badly, and I shall regret that always.

When I moved in with my aunt and uncle, I thought I had put all this behind me, and for five years I lived happily in my new home. But I soon found out that nothing is ever ideal when I began to have personal problems.

The first difficulty happened within my own body. It had been easy to be "good" when I had no sexual urges. But at twenty-five, a vigorous sex drive came to haunt me. Whenever I went out on a date, I had to use all my willpower to prevent myself from having sex.

Of course, the guys would have been willing. But it was wrong, what was happening to me. And my body did not discriminate. I felt sexy with almost every boy I dated. Then came the guilt, and it came with a vengeance. I punished myself mercilessly by truly believing that I was the most sinful person in the entire world.

At the same time, boredom set in at work. Doing the same job for five years became so automatic that it sent me into the humdrums. Dissatisfaction set in. For the first time, I began to dislike myself. My phobia, which had gotten progressively worse, was now in full bloom.

In desperation, I confided all my fears to my aunt. Ever since I was fourteen, my Aunt Sherry has been my best friend. I had shared with her all of my thoughts, and now I was in frantic need of understanding. I told her of my tremors. For reasons I could not understand, she turned a deaf ear to me.

Every time I tried to talk to her, she would get up and walk away. Or she would pick up a book and pretend to read. I could not believe it. My best friend had turned against me for reasons that were not my fault. Had I told her of Rey Littleton, she may have had a reason to turn away. But I only had explained my tremors to her.

That was the beginning of traumatic shock. At least that's what the doctor called it. The first stage of the illness was a rage so violent I could have killed her with my bare hands. I was standing behind her at the time, and I knew that I was strong enough at that time to put my hands around her throat and strangle her.

I had hardly shown any anger in my whole life, but at that point, it took all of my willpower to prevent myself from attacking her. My conscience won out, however, and all I managed to do was gasp.

The rage lasted for only a short time—one afternoon, in fact. Then, as suddenly as it came, it also subsided. In its place came a depression so deep that it was actual physical pain. The hurt and depression seemed to deepen with each passing day. I did not realize that I was ill. I only knew that I was hurt. Deeply.

There were scenes during my eight months of illness. I packed all my clothes at least twice and attempted to leave home. During those times, Sherry would convince me to stay, telling me that "my uncle would simply die if I ever left home."

Shock, hurt, and pain caused confusion. I could not eat because food would catch in my throat and I would be unable to swallow. And sleep meant endless nights of laying on my bed, unable to sink into unconsciousness, except for the terrible nightmares that waited for me.

Was it my imagination or did Aunt Sherry begin referring to Uncle Jeffrey as my husband? Once I caught a cold and was burning up with fever so bad I had to stay in bed for three days. She told me that my uncle was concerned about my cold. She conspicuously avoided the use of the first person singular, I.

When we sat down to eat at the table, she would boast about how beautiful my half sister Marla's hair was, upon which time my uncle would tell her how beautiful my hair was. This went on and on. If it wasn't my hair, it was my eyes or my figure. It would always have to be something about me that they could bicker about during dinner. The fact that she was jealous of me sent me into a panic and only made matters worse.

One day, my Aunt Sherry, whom I believed to be a religious woman, swore on the Bible in order to convince me that she was not angry with me, and I felt free of anxiety and happy for the entire afternoon. That evening though, my attempts at conversation only ended with failure. Why? What was the reason for this, I wanted to know. No answer. No explanation was given. It went on and on.

During my entire illness, I continued to work, although I missed many days on my job. It was a seventy-two-mile trek to Quonset Point each day. Once at work, I was conscious of others trying to help me. Because my body seemed to belong to someone else, when I typed I had to concentrate on moving each finger slowly and deliberately. My typing was so poor that my kind boss, Angelo Vitale, did my work for me. My legs were like rubber, and it took all of my concentration to make them walk.

The big boss's secretary took me to musicals twice and told me that I needed to get out more often and forget my problems. But listening to Liberace and Sam Martino did not help to ease the pressure. People sympathized, but no one knew how to help me because I said nothing about my situation to anyone. I felt that anything that I said about what was happening at home would be a betrayal of my aunt and uncle.

Even Uncle Jack, Sherry's brother who lived with us, gave me $2,000 to buy another car because my Metropolitan was badly in need of repairs. He told me that I had enough problems and that he did not want me worrying about money too.

Once, I tried going dancing, but I got propositioned so many times on the dance floor that it made me realize that I looked desperate. I felt dirty.

After that, my condition worsened. When people talked to me, their last words would repeat over and over in my head, forming a circle of words. It felt like my mind was not connected to my body. I felt intense pain and walked around in a daze.

I questioned whether or not I was losing my mind, but neither my aunt nor uncle suggested that I consult with a physician. Although suicide never entered my mind, I prayed constantly for God to take me. Anything was better than that pain.

Finally, one night, I had a nightmare that was so horrible that I could bear it no longer. I dreamed that I was impaled on a wooden cross, like Christ was. The cross was laying down rather than being upright, and Rickey, our pet German shepherd, was chewing off my hands and my feet. I felt it. I felt the flesh being torn off and saw the blood in his mouth. I awoke in a cold sweat, and the horror of it all convinced me to fight. I did not want to die a coward.

Since I was a small child, I had never turned to my mother for help. But that morning, I went to my mother's apartment, seeking comfort. Finding the door locked, I slumped down on the back seat of my car and waited in a suspended state of fear and anxiety for Mom to return from work.

That evening after hearing my story (which I had decided to tell to the world, no matter what the consequences), Mom called a psychiatrist and made an appointment for the following day. I looked like a skeleton, having lost a total of twenty-five pounds. I gave my mother $3 and asked her to get me a cheap bottle of wine so I would be able to sleep. Unaccustomed to alcohol, my body reacted to three tall glasses of wine, and I collapsed on the couch. I managed to get three hours of disturbed sleep.

The following day, I blurted out the whole story to the neurologist. The words came out in stuttering utterances. Dr. Stapens grabbed my hand and told me that I was suffering from shock and exhaustion. He took my car keys off me and told me that he was going to put me in Woonsocket General Hospital for a rest. I objected, telling him that I did not want to go to a crazy hospital. He then assured me that he was sending me there to keep watch over me.

Mom dropped me off at my aunt's house so I could pick up some clothes. I waited in the living room for her to come because I did not want to be in the company of my aunt. Uncle Jeffrey came into the room. At first he stood in the corner opposite mine.

He kept saying, as if to himself, that he did not care what the consequences were, and that he was going to tell me something. He crossed the floor, planted a firm kiss on my lips, and told me he loved me. I felt numb all over, wondered what he meant by this.

Still reluctant to go, yet unable to do anything about it, I let mom drive me to the hospital. When I arrived at the hospital wing which was reserved for the emotionally disturbed, I looked at my fellow inmates with suspicion.

Are these people crazy? Might they do me harm? As I glanced at the others in the suite, they all stared down at the floor, averting my gaze. Before I could decide whether or not I was safe, a nurse handed me a sleeping pill nicknamed the "red devil" and a pink tranquilizer.

They were so strong that my malnourished body literally fell asleep on my feet. The nurse and an attendant put me into bed. Once there, I slept for twelve hours. It was the first good night's sleep I had had in months. There were no nightmares. Only peace.

The next morning, the nurse asked me to remove all the bobby pins from my hair because I had a visit with the doctor. I could think straight. My mind was no longer fuzzy. Because the doctor was impressed with my clarity of speech, he canceled the electric shock therapy he had prepared me for.

I was drowsy and very hungry. For the next three days I slept around the clock, awaking only at meal time, when I ate ravenously like a starving wolf. The food was delicious. Never had food tasted so good. I savored each bite as it went down my throat. After eating, I would sleep again.

My sleep was fitful though. Once, I fell out of bed. On most mornings, the blankets were on the floor, and the bed was so messed up that the nurse had a tough time making it. She was a good nurse and poked fun at all of us patients.

She made a "doll" for me out of a pillowcase by stuffing it with cloth and tied a ribbon around its "neck" and told me that if I had someone to sleep with, maybe I would not joke so much. She also made fun of "Jack," another patient, by complaining constantly about his messy hair. Jack and I were mostly the butt of the jokes, but we enjoyed the teasing immensely.

Once the nurse, Agnes, suggested that I put cornflakes in Jack's bed so that he would wake up in the middle of the night, thereby enabling him to fix his hair. I complied. I put a whole box of cornflakes in his bed, which was way too much. But Jack didn't complain. He took the joke good-naturedly.

As to the "crazy" people I was afraid of at first, the patients in my wing were tremendous people. A school teacher, whose husband found collapsed on the floor from overwork was suffering from fatigue; a nun who came to the hospital periodically, suffering from depression; a woman who was trying to deal with the ramifications of divorce; and Jack, who told us that he had no idea that he was having a breakdown until his wife made him see a doctor.

We sat in the dayroom and listened to each other's problems, although I never volunteered any information about my case because I still was not able to share my secret with strangers.

The patient I was closest to, however, was "Arnold," a young, nice-looking boy who was suffering from schizophrenia. Arnold was undergoing electroshock treatments on a daily basis, and every day he would suffer memory loss regarding Jesus and the Bible. Since his religion was important to him, this distressed him immensely.

I took to explaining the love of Jesus to him each day. Before long, he was requesting that I take walks with him around the hospital, when we would talk about his problem at great length. Everyone on the ward was amazed that I could make him laugh, and he was happy when I was around.

After my third day of sleep, the doctor told me that I was well enough to drive again and I couldn't wait to sport my blue Chevrolet Impala around. I went on daily visits to Mom's house and remained there for most of the day, and every night, I would come running the walk barely in time for bed check, which was at ten o'clock.

Each time the patients would take odds to see whether or not I would make it back in time. I never failed though, and always barely made it. Agnes would wait at the door and pretend to be checking her watch with a not-to-convincing frown on her face, and my fellow patients thought that was hilarious. There was more laughter during my stay than there ever had been. And I was a happy person again.

My hospital confinement lasted for three weeks, and it was more like a vacation to me than a hospital stay. One morning, Dr. Stapens told me that I could return home and commented on my rapid recovery again.

CHAPTER 9

A changed woman emerged from that hospital visit. For one thing, I was no longer willing to listen to phrases like "nice girls don't do this, nice girls don't do that." After all, trying to be a nice girl had gotten me into problems at home. For another thing, I learned to trust my own judgment. I was a nice girl, and all that was important was for me to believe that, to know that, and no else's opinion mattered.

Getting out of the house, away from what I now called "the love triangle," was of prime importance. I called my sister and my friends, everyone my aunt had insisted that I not associate with, and let them know that no matter where they wanted to go and no matter what they wanted to do, I was willing to be a part of it.

Somehow, in the process of getting better, I had reached way back in my mind to childhood memories to a time when I had roamed the neighboring woods, to a time of independence, an independence that I had lost somewhere along the way, and I regained my freedom once more. I was my old self again, and knowing that brought me strength.

We frequented every nightclub we knew of and found others we had only heard rumors of. I danced and danced until two o'clock every morning and, afterward, would go out to eat in an after-hours restaurant.

I also rediscovered the laughter in my life that I had somehow lost during those staggering eight months of pain. I was commander of my own soul again, and I was in no hurry to surrender that post to anyone else soon.

One evening, about a month later, however, as I was leaving Eileen's lounge, in Pawtucket, "Louis" walked into my life again and asked if he could have a date. I told him "yes" but neglected to give him my telephone number on purpose because I really was not interested in meeting anyone. He followed me to Elsa's lounge, which was two blocks away, and made certain that he got hold of the number by being so polite and firm that I could not refuse.

Two day later, he was at my house with the oldest, ugliest automobile I had ever seen to take me to an exclusive nightclub for dinner and dancing. My aunt and uncle frowned when they saw the car, but I admired the audacity he had when he dared to pull this kind of stunt. The coupé was gray from lack of paint, dented on all sides, and the racket the muffler was making was so loud that we could hear it from the back of the house.

As I sat across the table from him, I took a long, hard look at this man for the first time and decided that I liked what I saw. His eyes were pleasant and intelligent looking, although his nose was rather large. I could tell by his speech that he was not very learned in books, but when he smiled, all that didn't seem to matter because he had straight even white teeth and lips that were begging to be kissed. He had a deep cleft in his chin that made my heart do flip-flops, and he wore his thick Italian hair combed back, which revealed his perfectly oval face. Why hadn't I dated this man before?

It was his enormous hands though, that made me feel strangely protected. It was the first time that I had experienced feelings of both sexual attraction and caring all rolled up together for one human being, and I didn't know quite what to make of it. I had never in my life felt both safe and yet excited like this before.

I sensed somehow that my entire future would depend on this man even though, when he proposed marriage on our third date, my answer had to be "not yet." I told him then of my three-week stay in a mental ward and the reasons that had led me there, and that I did not feel that I could handle marriage yet. Then I waited with bated breath for his response.

He said the magic words my heart had been hoping for. "Anyway you want it," he whispered in a kiss, "only don't leave me."

We took our time, and slowly, gradually, with this man I made new discoveries about life and about myself. I eventually realized that I had always been afraid of marriage because of my mother's bad experiences with it, and it was only because of Louis's kind and caring nature that I was able to think seriously of trusting my personhood to him.

Somehow I began to trust this man with those huge hands, even thought they could have easily clouted me like Dad had done to Mom. Something in my psyche demanded, needed a big, strong, tough guy to protect and care for me, yet somehow, deep inside, I feared what could happen if he didn't love me enough. Would I ever really and truly give my heart to this man? To any man, ever?

I "tested" him in a variety of ways. I met every one of his relatives and marveled that a prize such as he could come from a family that was so appalling. His older brother, "Junior," was an alcoholic and an impostor who cheated on his wife. His father, another alcoholic, compulsive gambler, and wife abuser lived in filth and squalor after his wife's death. Yet it was his sister who topped off this array of family horrors. I never realized before this that a woman could let herself go into such disrepair, both in her character and in her appearance.

He was not to blame for his upbringing, of course, and the fact that he was an upright, outstanding individual in spite of his drawbacks was amazing. The variety of friends of his began to explain things.

The first friends that I met were a married couple, Elbert and Lily Mantle from Scituate, Rhode Island. El enlightened me about Louis's circumstances before I ever asked. He told me that Louis was the best thing that had come from that family, except perhaps for his mother, who had died young.

She undoubtedly had been the positive influence on Louis's character. She had been a Roman Catholic nun before she married

Louis's father, who was an ex-convict, and had inspired Louis both in his moral fiber and his love for art.

Louis was in the process of building his mother her dream home when she died too young at fifty-seven. He was only nineteen years old at the time. On her deathbed she made him promise to take care of the entire family. He took his charge seriously and not only finished the house he had been building but, after his mother's death, also gave it to his brother when he got married.

He breathed a sigh of relief when his sister joined the navy, and he paid all the bills the family had owed. After getting disgusted with cleaning up the puke from one of his father's drunken escapades, Louis left him with $7,000 in cash and went out into the world to think only of himself for the first time in his life. He was then thirty-five years old.

Louis bought himself an apartment house in Providence and talked me into dating him a year later. Sam also informed me that Louis had saved him from drowning while they were in the national guards together. Louis had saved many lives while he was in the national guards. Once, when he was a sergeant in charge of a sixteen-millimeter canon crew, a shell misfired when the men were loading the gun. Louis grabbed the live shell, ran with it to the top of a hill, and threw it over the top. It exploded in midair.

From meeting his many friends, more evidence of his character began to emerge. He was the typical "good Samaritan," who was always helping someone who was in trouble. The many stories convinced me to fall in love with this remarkable man. I finally said yes to his marriage proposal three months later because I knew then I could trust him. The night we got engaged, he pounded the dashboard with one of his mighty hands. I was startled and asked him why he did that.

"You wasted seven years of our lives," he retorted.

My answer was simple. "I wasn't ready yet."

As to sex, I made a request of him, and it has taken me years to understand some of the reasons for this request. I told him I wanted to have intercourse with him before marriage, that I knew I would resist, if only because of a habit that I had formed throughout my dating life, but that I wanted to go through with it this time. I asked him to force me if necessary. This he did for me, for us and the manner in which he did it was both tender and forceful at the same time.

We had already made our wedding plans, set the date, and invited the guests. It was to be a simple church wedding in the Darlington Congregational Church in Pawtucket. My church.

Louis told me he wanted to show me the apartment he was getting ready for us in his Victorian house in Providence. It was on the second floor. He showed me the two large front rooms with the hard oak floors that he had lovingly polished. In the front parlor was an antique loveseat, newly upholstered in red and white tapestry.

The center room was a dining room, where he had placed an old dining table and six chairs. He had refinished and polished the table into a high luster. The Oriental rugs on the two floors led me to understand and appreciate his love for art and beauty.

The kitchen was furnished with a quaint breakfast set; the pantry was stocked with a complete set of dishes. He even had first aid supplies in the medicine cabinet.

Then he led me to the bedroom and ordered me to take off my clothes. I refused. He then tenderly and firmly began to do it for me. Then he laid me on the bed. That was how I found out what sex was all about. It hurt, and I bled.

Afterward, when I urinated, the toilet bowl turned crimson. It was a bit frightening to me because I had not expected so much blood. It was like having my monthly period. So that was it. That was all? Where was the big thrill I had always heard about? Oh well, I sighed to myself, if that was all there was to it, I figured I could put up with it once a week, even nightly if necessary.

I was happy to get it over with. At twenty-nine I suppose I had built up a fear of this thing called sex. Now I was not afraid anymore. Also, I know I had guilty feelings for the arousal I had experienced, not only with Louis but also with others, and now I felt that since I had given myself to Louis before we got married, I had also given him the chance to walk out on me if he wanted to.

In my idiotic way, I believed that this was fair somehow. I came home that night and secretly got the bloodstains off my panties before my aunt and then the entire world found out what I had done.

. . .

Marla looked lovely dressed in blue and carrying a bouquet of yellow roses. Everyone in my family had cautioned me not to let her be a part of my wedding party since she had a habit of spoiling things. But I was happy that I gave her the honor. She had always been a pretty girl, but now she glowed. Her eyes sparkled. I had borrowed the dress and had it tailored to fit her.

My aunt talked me into wearing a street-length gown of white lace, something that I shall always regret. I had admired the full-length gown I had tried on, and I should have bought that one instead. It was a simple wedding. Dad gave me away, and my white roses with a white orchid in the center shook as I marched down the aisle to become Mrs. Louis Robin Black.

Louis was uncharacteristically nervous, and I found out the reason why at the small reception which was held in the church basement. His family had come with the intentions of ruining my day.

His sister lit a cigarette in church and had to be told to put it out by the minister. Smoking was not allowed in church and she knew it. Louis knew they were up to something, but he did not know what they would do. This happened in retaliation for his not postponing the wedding because his Aunt Rose's third husband had passed away the week before.

We went on a skiing honeymoon in Vermont at Mt. Snow Ski Resort. We laughed at the cold water faucet in our bathroom that never shut off; we laughed at the couple in the room next to ours who never smiled; we laughed at the squeak in our mattress whenever we tried to make love. The whole wide world was full of joy for us. And after our honeymoon was over, I discovered the climax for the first time in our apartment. Sex was worth waiting for after all.

It was time again to leave insanity behind, to escape from its clutches, and to go happily into the future with this man of mine. I felt almost as if I was being born anew. The time had come for me to forget the past, to blot it out of my memory forever, and to move ever onward.

CHAPTER 10

Living in the big city was new and strange to me. One day, while sitting in our car waiting for the butcher shop to open, Louis and I watched three young children rob a mom 'n pop grocery store.

They had a system worked out whereby one would get the owner's attention, and his partner in crime would grab a loaf of bread or something else, while the third youngster would engage the owner in a conversation. Then the three of them would run down the street, giggling with their confiscated booty. They couldn't have been more than six or seven years old. Hindsight tells me that we should have reported the incident, but it was probably their age that stopped us.

At any rate, we were determined that our children would not be reared in Providence, so we began house hunting as soon as we married. I had been brought up in the country, and our children would have the advantage of the woods to play in, a pond to swim in, and a small country school to attend.

When we found a lovely old farmhouse in Scituate that had been newly renovated, we decided to take a chance on a mortgage. It was situated on nine and a half wooded acres. The eleven-room house presented a perfect setting for the antique shop we planned on operating there.

I was pregnant when we moved in, and my husband, who was concerned with my health and that of the baby, refused to let me help with the moving. Those giant, wonderful, and powerful hands were always there to protect and care for my unborn baby and me. I don't believe that many woman received the care and adoration that I did.

. . .

Twin baby boys came into this world thirteen months after we were married. The surprise baffled me, but not Louis. He had insisted all along that it was going to be two babies because of the size of my huge belly. Besides there were twins on both sides of our family. It was a difficult birth for both them and me.

I was in labor for thirty-six hours, and they were six weeks premature. I was concerned for their health. In order to allay my fears, the obstetrician had them tested for brain damage and found none. The older by ten minutes I named Louis Junior and the younger, of course, was named Samuel Charles after my older brother.

They were big for premature babies. Louis weighed five pounds and two ounces, and Samuel missed the five-pound mark by two ounces.

It was not until two nurses wheeled the incubators into my hospital room that I was satisfied that they were normal, even though I was not allowed to touch them. I counted all ten fingers and ten toes on each of my pink baldheaded darling infants when I was allowed to see them. My twin cherubs were perfect, and they demanded most of my attention for the next four years.

They were unusual children from the beginning. Nothing in the house was safe from these healthy, active infants. By the time they were three months old, their stomachs were distended because I had fed them too much formula.

Upon seeing what was happening, I took them to a pediatrician who told me they weren't getting enough nourishment. She suggested feeding them roast beef. After that, I tried putting the tip of a baby spoon into a jar of baby food roast beef at bedtime. It worked. Satisfied, they were sleeping for three hours at a time.

At this time we had a pond dug in the backyard. It was a beautiful pond. We also stocked it with largemouth bass. It had a continuing water supply, which meant it would never get polluted.

By the time the babies were eight months old, they had torn their cribs apart. On one occasion, when I entered their bedroom, I found the twins fencing with spokes they had torn from their cribs. On another occasion, Lou threw his glass bottle across his bedroom, and it crashed through a window.

Nighttime was a challenge in the Black household. The boys spent most of infanthood on mattresses that were on the floor because they were not big enough to sleep in a bed. The baseboards in the room were secured to the floor by two-by-four planks because they had cut their tiny fingers trying to take them apart.

Baby gates were no match for them. Squealing with delight like little gremlins, they would rock back and forth, back and forth, leaning on it with their full weight, until the gate fell apart. Louis had to nail boards across the doorway of their room. Once they climbed over these boards though, the entire house was not safe.

Once, in the middle of the night, they escaped from their room, crawled down the stairs, opened the refrigerator, got out a roast beef that I had prepared that day, and were chewing on it before I could stop them.

Another time, they managed to get hold of the flat iron (which I had set to cool in the corner of the kitchen counter). In order to do this, they had to take one of the living room chairs and move it into the kitchen. Then they took the iron into the parlor and plugged it in. Samuel woke me up when he burned his hand.

"Boo, boo," he cried as he climbed into our bed. Immediately I smelled something burning. I raced downstairs and found the hot iron burning a hole in the floor.

But Louis did not give up. To keep them from harm, he made a strap. The twins watched him do it. Wide-eyed, they looked on as he fastened the end of a leather belt with the buckle cut off around in a loop and attached it to a wooden handle and hung it high on a nail in the kitchen.

After that they behaved. The strap was never intended to be used—only as a threat. Indeed, after the strap was made, they were so well mannered that people used to remark about how polite they were.

One day, years later, the strap disappeared. Louis and Sam got the sacred object down and burned it in the trash barrel.

Mirror twins. I first heard that phrase shortly after they were born, and it aptly applied to them. Lou, for some reason, cried most nights, probably because he was always hungry. Impatient Samuel, by contrast, cried most of the day.

Whenever one seemed to be happy, the other would always have problems. Lou was left-handed; Sam was right-handed. Lou was shy and withdrawn while Sam embraced all the visitors and customers who came into our home with tiny open arms.

The toughest job I ever had was raking care of those twins. It wasn't the work that wore me out, although washing cloth diapers when we had no dryer meant that I had to string clotheslines throughout the kitchen-living room area. The glass bottles had to be sterilized twice a day and there was constant cleaning and feeding and changing and bathing.

Their crying made me nervous, and I was hemorrhaging most of the time, so I needed to keep my mind off the crying. I still am amazed at the work I accomplished during the first four years after their birth.

I found time to make braided rugs, to refinish furniture, refinish the old wide board floors in the dining and living rooms, design and sew draperies and curtains for all twenty-eight windows in the entire house, paint and decorate all eleven rooms, and that's not all.

I upholstered furniture and made all my own clothes. Once, because we had no money to purchase gifts at Christmas outside of our own home, I knitted gloves for the entire family out of some yarn Louis had discovered in his mother's old hope chest. That was nine pairs of gloves in all.

It seemed like simple therapy to me. When the babies cried and I couldn't pacify them, I worked. But it became too much for me. On one occasion, when I brought the babies to the doctor for their check up, I cried all over the place in the doctor's office and confessed that I had not gotten a decent night's sleep in four years.

I must've looked a pitiful sight to Dr. DiPippo. I was very skinny. My eyes were bloodshot, and the veins were popping out on the back of my hands. He reached in his desk drawer and pulled out a bottle of pills that he handed to me.

"These will help you to sleep," he told me.

I came home from the office visit, put the babies to bed for their afternoon nap, took one pill, and got three hours of blessed sleep myself. The pills worked! I couldn't believe that those tiny triangular anti-depressants could perform such a miracle in my life, but they did.

The house was still polished because I cleaned all the downstairs floors on my hands and knees every week, but the weight I gained because of the ten-hour sleep I was getting every night made it possible for me to work even harder. Also the hemorrhaging subsided. I did not connect my heightened energy with mental illness, but it was a part of bipolar disease, also called manic-depression. I was a sick woman and never suspected it.

Along with my regained health, I began to enjoy my two little angels more. Having twins can be twice the fun. They now each had a rocking horse, which we kept in the den upstairs, next to the bedrooms. One night, we heard a wee voice say, "Mommy, can I go tinkle?"

After the request was granted, we watched one painted pony mysteriously edge its way toward their bedroom. We heard the request again from another voice, and the whole process was repeated, while Louis and I stifled fits of laughter. The next morning, the two little darlings were sleeping beside their "horsies."

They walked early and talked late. I assumed that they were not too bright because of their retarded speech, but I learned later that the only reason they didn't talk was because they had no reason to.

They had developed a means of communicating between the two of them, which satisfied them both.

I was convinced now that insanity had been left way behind when I had left my family and the state of Massachusetts miles away, and I experienced a happiness that I never thought was possible for me.

My brother Jack, or Junior, had married and had three children. We didn't see too much of him, but I was satisfied that he and his family were normal. The only improvement that could have enhanced my happy life more would have been that my husband could have shown the children and me more affection. It just was not in him. Something was missing somewhere, and I approached him about it on several occasions.

"Louis," I told him, "the children need to know that you love them. Pick them up, and hold them once in a while."

The only answer I received was something like, "Of course, I love them. I work two jobs in order to provide a roof over their heads and food on the table. That's love. Many men tell their wives and kids they love them, but then they cheat and drink and take the food out of their children's mouths. I don't."

He was right. I saw him go to work with holes in his shoes in order to give us the best that he could. To compensate for his lack of affection, I gave the twins lots of love. I was always picking them up and rocking and hugging them. I was so happy with my babies that, when they were four years old, I wanted another one.

It would be nice to have a girl. At first, Louis would not agree to it because he was afraid I might get sick again. But eventually, I got my own way; we tried for three months and were successful. Jonathan Luigi Black was born November 30, 1972, approximately five years after his brothers.

"Jonathan" was nothing like his brothers. Although he was my biggest baby at birth, it soon became apparent that he was going to be a small man. He had his assets though. He was far handsomer then his older siblings, although he would never have their wide shoulders.

I called him my "love child," because right from the beginning it was a joy taking care of him. He rarely cried, and every time I checked up on him in his crib, he would always give me a big smile. The only problem I had with Jonathan was he got into everything. He had an active mind that led him into many dangerous situations. He was a very difficult child to watch.

He was fascinated with Louis's shaving and used to watch him every time he would go into the bathroom. But being an onlooker was not enough for him. One night, when we were sound asleep, he crawled downstairs, pulled over a chair, climbed up to the bathroom vanity, and was playing with the blades. He woke me up when his fingers were bleeding. Fortunately, only the tips of his fingers were scarred.

One time, when I was studying, he found a jar of gold leaf paint that my husband had left behind the drapes in the dining room. When he came to me, his lips were gold rimmed from the paint. I picked him up and rushed him to Rhode Island Hospital, where they worked on him for hours, trying to get him to regurgitate. Nothing worked.

They tried to pump his stomach, gave him something to make him vomit, and an enema. But nothing worked. They finally sent him home in the middle of the afternoon. After ten minutes of driving him home, the motion of the automobile cause him to vomit and pass diarrhea at the same time. I pulled the car over and cleaned up the mess with a roll of paper towels I always kept in the car.

This happened twice on the way home. Once I got him home, I gave him a bath and set him on his little rocking horse. He messed again all over the place, and I had to clean him up again. Finally the vomiting was over. A caring doctor called that night and wanted to know if Jonathan had vomited, and he was very relieved when I told him he did.

Another time, I left him alone for a few minutes in order to dig out a plant in my backyard. My husband was working in the garage, so I figured that door was guarded. When I returned, he was gone. Louis had left the garage and was working on the side of the house. That left Jonathan unattended.

He got out of the house, ran down the driveway and into the middle of the road. When I found him, a man had gotten out of his car and was stopping all the traffic. Jonathan was dressed only in his diaper when I snatched him up.

"Lady, why don't you watch your kid," the angry man yelled at me as I ran into the house with my precious cargo.

There were other times when my son got into things. I had the poison control number to Rhode Island Hospital at my fingertips and used it on two occasions.

In spite of all this, Jonathan was a delight to be with. He was active and cried little. And he also was very intelligent. By the age of two he was reasoning. He was very verbal and was walking by eleven months.

Jonathan brought Louis and me more happiness. As he grew, his active mind took an interest in a variety of things: the woods and wildlife and nature in all its aspects. He hated school like my brother Jack. Jonathan had to be made to go to school, and this wasn't easy.

When Jonathan was only a year old, I went back to school to get a degree. At this time I decided to adopt, and my husband agreed to it. We went through nine months of a "home study" in order to fulfill the requirements. Even though I was thirty-seven years old and was still capable of giving birth, they wanted us to adopt an older child because of our age.

Louis went to New York City by bus to pick "Louis Angel" up, and she became part of our family when Jonathan was two years old. I had been told that the weather in New England would be cold for her, so I bought her a jacket and put two small dolls in a pocket for her to play with on the way home.

She could only speak one word of English when she came to us. She had learned how to say "candy" on the long trip from Korea. I now had a daughter who was six years old. My family was complete.

We adopted her two weeks before Thanksgiving, and the first words she learned were the different types of food. After being used to one bowl of rice a day at the orphanage, her eyes opened wide when she saw me serve the Thanksgiving meal.

That Christmas I thought she would bust wide-open with joy. She got a small table and chairs to put her new dolls in and a tea set, among other things. I will always remember that Christmas as being one of the happiest I ever had in my life.

Angel learned how to speak English very quickly and was soon in school with her older brothers.

But tough times loomed on the horizon. Although my husband was a hard worker, we never had enough money because food and energy bills were high. He was a construction foreman, and because jobs in construction were very unstable in Rhode Island, he always worked at another job as well. Even though I managed the household with little funds and brought in an extra paycheck myself, we were forced to go on welfare on two occasions.

Being in poverty bothered Louis so much that by the age of forty-five, he became a bitter and depressed man. It was impossible for me to make him happy. He brooded constantly because he believed that life had passed him by. All of his friends had money in the bank and he felt inadequate because his bank account reflected the fact that he was poor.

But I knew that his biggest talent was in art, so I convinced him at the darkest hour of his life to do some artwork.

"Louis, I've always wanted a portrait of our home," I told him. "Do you remember when you used to paint in grammar school? Could you do this painting for me now?"

He not only made the painting, but he took art lessons as well, which brought some measure of success into his life. He made paintings and wood sculptures, which he sold, to passersby. They have since dotted the landscapes of many towns throughout the United States.

Working on his carving brought him out of his depression. A year after we went on welfare, we made so much money that we gave more to charity than what we received from the government.

Louis was a creative man. He could see the world differently than everyone else. He saw beauty in the hardened face of an old sea captain and in the ugly face of an old woman. His statues sold almost as fast as he made them. He was making a statue every week. And he was happy now with his new career.

I went back to school and got a BA degree in education five and a half years after Jonathan's first birthday. And I graduated with honors. It opened up new doors for me and for my family because the whole family was turned on by my interest in books. I spent hours talking to and teaching my children, and the books I bought them contributed greatly toward the enhancement of their lives.

CHAPTER 11

While my life was happy and full, my sister's was all going downhill. On top of mixing drugs and alcohol, she began having sex with all kinds of men that she met in nightclubs. And she didn't discriminate. Some of them were married, and all of them were unscrupulous characters.

On one occasion she was "gang raped." One guy drove her into the woods where a gang of guys was waiting. After tearing off her clothes, they all took turns raping her. Then they left her to find her way home as best as she could. Fortunately the woods were not too far from the nightclub. She half crawled, half walked to her car.

In spite of all this, she frequented barrooms often, even though she was jeered at and ridiculed. She was trying to satisfy her tremendous sex drive. Her entire family rejected her, even me. Mom was the only friend she had.

We all breathed a sigh of relief when Herman Johnson entered her life. He was different than all the other guys even though she met him in a nightclub too. "Herm" was a big man by anyone's estimation. He respected her, and he loved her. He also understood her illness because he had taken care of his sick mother all his life.

Going out with him kept her out of nightclubs, and it seemed for a while that she might have been slated for happiness after all. Her boyfriend doted on her and treated her to lavish dinners. He bought her beautiful clothes and jewelry and spent a great deal of time with her, trying to make her happy. She glowed with all that attention.

"I'd like to marry Herm," she told me often, and it seemed that that might happen someday. He was well liked by the family. The relationship lasted for seven years, and when Jonathan was born, I asked them to be his godparents.

However, Marla was not meant to be happy for long. She still needed pills. One night, unable to sleep, she called Dr. Benjamin, a family practitioner who still went on house calls. She had done this several times before.

"Please come over and give me a shot to make me sleep," she begged.

"I'll give you a shot only if you haven't taken any pills today," he cautioned when he arrived at the house.

She lied, "I haven't taken any—not one."

Indeed, she had taken seven pills that day, three more than what the prescription had allowed. She had always been neurotic and plagued by fears and lethargy. She was even an addict. But not until that eventful night did she totally become psychotic. No one but the doctor knew for sure what was in that shot, but that night for the first time she began to imagine strange things.

The next morning, Herm took her to my house. Mom was working and he didn't know what to do with her. He had to go to work himself.

Her eyes were wild. "I've had twins," she yelled. "Twin boys. Do you know me?" she raved. She kept repeating that she had twins. The only semblance this had to reality at all was the fact my firstborn babies were twins. It seemed that her twisted mind thought she was me.

I bit my tongue. In the heat, the odor of my sister's body clung to my nostrils. My heart seemed to leap into my throat. I should have been used to these kinds of calamities, but somehow I got frightened every time.

"It's a good thing the children are sleeping," I decided. I wouldn't want them to see something like this. I had to calm down and think clearly. Marla was hollering again about the twins.

"You'd better enter her into a hospital, Herm. It's not safe to let her stay alone, and she can't stay here. God knows what she might do."

At the age of thirty-five, after a turbulent life, Marla admitted herself into a mental hospital. There they put her in a padded cell, naked, until all the drugs were out of her system. It was only for a brief stay. Too brief. Although she was still disoriented, she was out in two months. Afterward she returned to live with Mom.

But the incident caused Herm to have second thoughts. Because his mother's illness had led her to an early grave, now the thought of marrying a sick woman was unbearable. As time went on, he began to seek the company of other women. Eventually, he met someone new. When it came time to tell Marla of this, he cried openly because he still loved her.

"I've found someone else," he sobbed. "Even though I'll always love you, there's no future for us. I'm going to marry this girl."

Marla's mouth hung open. "But Herm, I can't believe it. Why, you love me, not her. You can't leave me."

Herm walked away from her then. In the weeks and months that followed, she was alone again. After he left, her condition worsened. Because she had a love/hate relationship with mom, the more her mother did for her, the more she resented it.

One day she released all her fury on my mother.

"Ahhh," she screamed like a madwoman. She flung open the kitchen cabinets and smashed all the dishes on the floor. Then she grabbed one of the kitchen chairs and threw it down the stairs. She grabbed another, then another. One by one, she threw them after the first until a chair broke into pieces.

Her anger wasn't satisfied until she picked up a chair in the parlor and smashed it into the new television set. Then, she pushed her mother.

"You're to blame for all this," she screamed.

Mom went into shock. Her hands began to shake. Her heart pounded too loudly, it seemed as if her chest would pop open. She managed to reach for the phone and dialed Junior's telephone number.

Junior got there as quickly as he could. When he arrived, he saw his disturbed mother trying to sweep up the mess with a broom. He called the police. When they came, Marla was still ranting and raving. She didn't seem to know where she was.

"It's her fault," she kept yelling at the top of her lungs. The police took her to a hospital.

Jack Junior cleaned up the mess for his mother. Then he called his older sister. When Louis and I arrived, we saw that my mother was suffering from shock. Her face was twisted to one side and she was hysterical. She was sobbing and out of control.

"Ma," I convinced my mother, "come stay with us. We'll fix up the loft so you can have a nice apartment upstairs. We'll take care of you. You can't live with Marla anymore."

My defeated mother agreed. "All right, Ruth. I don't know what I did wrong. I always try to do the best thing."

Her only crime was that she loved her daughter too much. She would never understand why it all had happened.

. . .

When I took Mom in to live with me, I knew that she needed a job more than anything else. She had to be kept busy. I checked the local newspaper and saw that there was an opening for foot press operators at a nearby factory. Three days after she moved in with me, I took her there to apply for a position. Because Mom's hands were shaking so badly, I filled out the application form for her.

"How soon can you start work, Mrs. Midsummer?" the secretary wanted to know.

Mom looked at me for an answer, and I quickly replied, "As soon as possible."

In the months that followed, Mom's nerves became progressively better. Work had always agreed with her, and with a healthy atmosphere around her, she gradually responded to the kindness.

In turn, she was a comfort to the entire family. Playing with her grandchildren, who soon totaled four, brought her joy. She often bought goodies and presents that my budget didn't allow for.

Also, her financial situation took a turn for the better when she filed for disability for Marla. She got it. No longer would she have to support her sick daughter. Marla was better off as well. At last, committed to a mental hospital, she received some help. She was tested and the doctors diagnosed her as being schizophrenic and suffering from convulsions.

Because they decided that her illness could better be treated in a group home, after a few months they transferred her to a group home in Massachusetts. However, that didn't work out to everyone's satisfaction. Once there, she was very difficult to live with because she refused to obey orders. Because of that they decided that they couldn't help her. She was then sent to another group home in Norton, Massachusetts, where she stayed for two years.

Shortly afterward, Mom had her transferred to the Institute of Mental Health (IMH) in Cranston, Rhode Island, near where I made my home. She wanted to keep her daughter close by so she could visit more often. There, for the first time, doctors had some success in straightening out her distorted personality.

When the head psychiatrist at the IMH read Marla's medical records, he cried. As he wiped his eyes, he realized that her whole environment had predetermined that her life would end in failure. Frightened as a young child, and coddled by a doting mother, she had been hurt in as many ways as possible.

When people opened up doors for my sister, she closed every one. At the hospital, she often misbehaved in a big way. Once again, she threw a heavy oak chair through a television set, this time in her hospital wing. Because of that, she was not allowed to have visitors for months.

During her entire illness, Marla had to bear intense emotional anguish. Her thoughts were disturbed. She was in constant agony, and tears streaked down her cheeks more often than not. Because she looked at the world through a sick mind, her view of it was distorted.

Although she loved her mother dearly, she nevertheless blamed her in part for her illness. As the authorities at the IMH had already determined, her tortured mind could not reason well enough so that she could live safely in society, even though her mother was allowed to visit her often.

In spite of all that, they let her loose. They had to. Because of legalities, she could not be kept there against her will. Since she had signed herself in, the law said she could sign herself out.

Furthermore, at that time the state was experimenting with deinstitutionalization. Marla was intelligent enough to know this, so she went to the head doctors and requested that she be released. Because they legally had no choice and because the state wanted to get rid of as many patients as possible, they unlocked the doors and set her free.

Marla found herself out on the streets with only a few dollars in her pocket and no place to stay. Of course, she phoned her mother.

"Ma," she said excited, "they let me out. I'm in the city, and I need a place to stay. See if Ruth will let me live with her."

At first, Mom couldn't believe it. Then a flicker of hope came into her mind. She had never given up the dream of living with Marla again, and she saw this as a chance to make it happen.

She had lived with us for seven years, and in all that time she brought a lot of joy to the house. My children loved her very much, and I had done everything to make my mother happy. But when she asked me to let Marla move in with us, my answer had to be no. I was torn. I loved my mother, but Louis and the children had to come first. Their happiness was at stake.

I had to refuse my mother's request. That didn't discourage Mom. Her mind finagled a way of letting her dream come true. She had an elderly cousin named Jean who lived alone. She contacted her, and Jean was more than happy to comply. She was suffering from Alzheimer's disease, and now she would have someone to live with. Mom again had a purpose in life. She had two sick people to care for.

Not for long. True to tradition, Marla acted up again. This time when she got angry, she not only shoved Mom but also knocked Jean to the floor. The police came, and Marla was forced to admit herself into a mental hospital, this time back in the state of Massachusetts. Once there, attendants watched her closely again. They monitored her every move.

At times she seemed almost normal. She could reason to some extent, and her memory was remarkable. Because of this, doctors again decided that she would function well in a group home with the proper medication and psychiatric care.

I finally decided to ask myself questions. Why did my brother Samuel remain hopelessly psychotic, and why was my sister unable to live in society? Was this an illness that was unique to my family? Was it in fact inherited? Was it in our genes? If it was inherited, then why was my brother Jack and I spared the effects of this disease? Then I realized, from looking back over my lifetime, that I did in fact become ill three times myself: once when Raymond Perez tried to shoot us, once during the love triangle thing, and once after my twins were born. And what about my brother Jack. He worked harder than most men did. And he consumed a six-pack of beer a day. Was alcohol medicine for him?

Also, why did this happen in my family alone? Of the 108 cousins on my mother's side of the family, only one became mentally ill. My cousin Ellen had a nervous breakdown because of her alcoholic husband. Yet all four of my mother's children had psychiatric problems? Why were we singled out?

To be sure, every one of Granny's children had some sort of mental illness in one form or another, that is, all but the ones who died young. My oldest uncle Steven became ill after he made that invention for the Corning Glass company, Aunt Sarah spent years in a mental hospital, Uncle Sidney became ill after his wife became pregnant. That was the reason they decided to have only one child.

My uncles George and Herman and my Aunt Terry were all alcoholics. Both of my aunts Carol and Amanda became ill when they found out that their husbands were cheating on them, and both of them had to be put in a mental hospital for their illnesses. Uncle Luigi spent his entire life in Taunton State Hospital for the Mentally Ill.

Then, of course, there was my unlucky mother. Three of Granny's and Grandpa's children died too young to get sick. One was killed in a train accident when he was only ten years old. That was my Uncle Samuel. Another uncle, Uncle Otto, died at age twenty-eight from bone cancer. That only left Uncle Norman who died as an Infant.

The family tree on my mother's side was riddled with some form of mental illness or another. But why was it only my mother's children affected and not my cousins? That common denominator had to come from my father's side of the family. My father must have some form of mental illness, although he would never admit it. Yet his bottle of booze was his constant companion. Also, he did get sick after my mother left him

The pattern was coming in clearer in my mind. Both of my parents were candidates for mental illness. That was why we four children had it.

The dedicated professionals, social workers, psychiatrists, psychologists, and other who worked with Marla for long hours tried to help her as best as they could. They faced frustrations, not only because their resources were limited but also without cooperation from my mother, her life could not have been steered in the right direction.

Marla had to be made to help out at home. There were plenty of things she could have done around the house. Being the baby of the house, she was given no motivation. I mistakenly blamed her entire illness on her laziness and lack of motivation. That simply was not so. Yet if she had only tried to do something around the house to help her mother, I am convinced that she would have fared better.

As to the role that my mother played in all this, she may have blamed herself for Samuel's illness and was fearful that if she didn't cater to every whim that my sister had, then she would get as sick as Sam did. Her entire life had been wrapped up in caring for two sick children. Ironically, the worst thing that had ever happened to Marla was that she lived with her mother after she had reached maturity.

Nevertheless, the staff at the home began to let Marla come home on weekends. This alarmed me and my sister-in-law Barbara, my brother Jack's wife. We saw this as a threat to Mom's health. We feared that, before long, Marla would be let loose in her mother's custody, and the abuse would start all over again.

To counteract that, I tried to get legal custody of my sister in order to prevent it from happening. I also had a meeting with my sister-in-law.

"We must do something about this. Perhaps we can go to the authorities. We can't let the two of them live together."

Joan agreed. And I hired a lawyer. But it wasn't all that easy. Legally, it was impossible, the lawyer informed me. A long, involved court battle would have only proved to be costly. I was grateful that it wasn't necessary. Instead, the two of us had a conference with the social workers that were in charge of the group home.

"Marla can't possibly live with her mother," we both stated in unison. "It would be the worst possible thing that could happen to them."

Then they made provisions whereby, for the time being at least, Marla would only be allowed to stay with Mom on weekends.

But the group home was discontinued two years from the time Marla had been admitted. Again, she was transferred. This time the home was located on Division Street in North Attleboro.

The actions of mental patients can be totally unpredictable. One night, while Marla was in bed, in spite of all the precautions that the staff took, a male patient got out of his room at night and raped both her and her roommate.

Marla was a fighter. "You can't do this," she screamed. She punched and kicked violently. The man got more than he bargained for. She beat him up and, in the scuffle, managed to tear his clothes. Marla was bleeding from her mouth because the man was choking her, trying to prevent her from yelling for help. And she was also bleeding from her vagina.

While the incident was upsetting for Marla, it was worse for her roommate, who slashed her wrists. Both of the women were sent back to Taunton again. The man was disciplined and locked up for a while.

Because of all the commotion that was caused by the event, Mom and Marla had to appear in court. There, in the presence of the judge, not one of the workers at the home mentioned the rape. Mom and Marla were silent as well.

"I was afraid to cause any trouble," Mom told me. The whole incident was swept under the rug. A few months later, the rapist was released from the group home.

CHAPTER 12

The twins were unusually bright and creative right from the start, and while in the fifth grade, for the first time in grammar school, they were put in the same classroom. There, their teacher, Mrs. Chatalian, recognized their genius and enlisted them into the gifted children's program.

Their creative talents must have come from their father because both boys excelled in art and were able to see and come up with innovative ideas not thought up by anyone previously.

Paper towel cardboard became rocket ships, and empty toilet paper rolls became submarines. They not only excelled in academics but also often made graphs, maps, games, and artworks just for the fun of it, in addition to the requirements of the school curriculum. They got their homework done in between classes so they could do their own projects at home.

Mrs. Chatalian made me see the fact that they should be headed for college. "It would be a terrible waste not to let them use their talents," she told me.

Twins are unique, especially identical twins. And raising Louis and Samuel was a special challenge. If the thought that mental illness was in my genes had ever occurred to me at the time I was planning on having a family, I probably would never have had children. But when my two boys went to junior high school, the old family monster, the curse, came back again to crush my children and me.

All the attention that they received from Mrs. Chatalian could have caused some jealousy because, during junior high, it seemed that most of the kids were against them. They stood apart from the others because, (1) they were very bright, (2) they were also well-mannered (something which most students lacked), (3) they didn't use profanity, (4) they were awkward in most social situations, and (5) we were too poor to buy them designer jeans or Nike sneakers.

The story I got from Samuel about his first days of school goes as follows: "We were waiting outside in front of the house for the bus. I remember I was only twelve. I was going to junior high. Someone in the house said this is the big boy school, don't be afraid. I was happy. It was at a different time, early in the morning.

"The big school bus was coming. Louis got on the bus first. It was a sunny day. Louis moved down the aisle pretty close to me. The second seat was open. As I started to walk, someone's hand grabbed my arm. Someone hissed, 'Save that seat for my girlfriend.' I was okay with that. I thought he just wanted me to do him a favor. Then this girl got on the bus after a lot of other people. She came in, and her boyfriend grabbed her coat and told her to go get her seat.

"Then he said to me, 'You, get out.' Like a dumb idiot I said, 'What?' I got out of the chair, and he punched me right in the face. I was shorter then. I started to cry, and everyone started to call me a crybaby. That was the beginning of junior high for me.

"I found a seat on the back of the bus. I never sat in front of the bus after that. I was able to triple up, three people in a seat. The bus driver never saw one incident, and there were hundreds of things that happened to us on the bus.

"Another time, we were all sitting outside. This is high school, the first day. During our first break, someone threw a small rock and hit me on my lower back. I was bleeding. I have a scar there today. I turned around and found that it was one of my friends who did it.

"His name was Joe Shmo. He said, 'Come on, stand up. The Black babies are sissies.' I was afraid, scared to death. It would take me another year to learn how to hide. He was saying 'Come on, what are you going to do about it? The Black boys are a bunch of sissies and babies.'

"I didn't cry that time because I was too used to being on the watch for danger. It could come from anywhere: a stone, a punch, a kick, a spitball, a taunting remark. You had to be ready to run. I learned how to run, and Louis learned how to fight."

More bad things continued to happen. About a week after school started, Samuel was knocked off his bicycle by a punk one day when school was over. Louis and "Sam" were riding their new bicycles down the side of the road when the kid, Paul Jilson, who was older and bigger, stopped them for no apparent reason, and began to punch Sam and Louis. Louis was clutching a tire iron in his fist and was prepared to use it if necessary.

The attack was so vicious that a passing motorist parked his car and chased the boy away. Sam never quite got over the incident, which not only damaged him physically but emotionally as well.

My husband wanted to go to school the next day and complain to the principal, but the boys stopped him.

"We'll handle it ourselves, Dad," Louis told him. "If we tell on him, we'll be known as snitches. Don't worry, we'll be all right."

But other things began to happen. One day Samuel came home with another story.

"Today, my third day in high school, someone pushed my face into a toilet. The toilet had feces in it. It took four of them to do this. They shoved my face in the piss. I think they made me drink some of it. I know I got some of it in my mouth.

"A kid named Alfonse Smart one day wanted my apple juice. He said his was not fresh. He wanted mine. So I took his and started drinking it, and I found out it was urine. The whole school busted out laughing. This happened in the cafeteria.

"There were more practical jokes than physical encounters. More psychological torture and social rejection. These things happened ten times a day.

"I lost a fight at the end of that day. Every two weeks there was a real fight for both Louis and me. I was called every name in the book by all the kids, and I wasn't allowed to participate in anything. We were always picked last in everything; nobody wanted us on the team. We were put out in left field."

That's when the social and psychological isolation began.

Louis began to get into fistfights often because he was tormented too by the girls as well as the boys. Although he would hit back at the guys who punched him, he would never strike a girl.

One day he was in tears. "Mom, today during English class, a girl kept poking me in the back with a pen. There was nothing I could do about it because she was a girl. She kept it up and kept it up during the whole period. I couldn't study."

"Why didn't you tell the teacher?" I asked him.

"Oh, the teachers never listen to me. They think I'm a troublemaker."

Louis was obviously upset. He didn't cry often. I didn't know what to think of all this. But one week, Sam, who was the talkative twin, refused to talk for the first time in his life. He spent two weeks in a depressed state and wouldn't talk to anyone.

Because he had always been a verbal child from infancy, his silence awakened me to the fact that something was terribly wrong. I remembered that my brother Samuel stopped talking right before he withdrew into himself. It was alarming.

Also, when I received his next report card, I was alarmed again. He was failing in many of his classes. I managed to get the story from a frightened Sam, who didn't know himself what was going on.

"Mom," he painfully told me. "Last week I got an A+ on a biology test. The teacher, who always announces test grades, praised me in front of the entire class. I was very happy because it's not too often that anything good ever happens to me.

"But the next day, Jim Turk (Louis's best friend) stood in front of the classroom when the teacher had stepped out of the class, and ridiculed Louis and me. He boasted, 'We're all going to take a collection and buy you a new pair of Nikes. Your mother buys cheap clothes from K-Mart.'

"'Also, you need haircuts. Your hair looks lousy. And you stink. You never take a shower.' All his pals in the classroom began to laugh."

With that, Samuel burst into tears. "You know I've been taking a bath every day. Why don't the kids like us?" Sam withdrew socially from girls after that happened.

I felt guilty. I had been giving the boys haircuts myself to save money.

This was so serious that I convinced Louis to visit the school with me. There, my angry husband pounded his fist on the principal's desk and roared, "Something has to be done. My son is a bright boy. Why is he failing in all of his classes? We don't have to put up with this shit!"

The principal, Mr. Chandler, realized that this was something the school authorities couldn't ignore. He set up a meeting. The teachers, social worker, and school psychiatrist came to talk to us at the principal's office.

The first step the school officials decided to take was to separate the twins. They changed their schedules and placed them in different classes. Being separated, they would not be as conspicuous.

Then, they tested their IQs. As was suspected, the results showed that the scores were higher than average. A week later, the school psychiatrist evaluated them.

Her report was alarming. I had been so concerned about Sam that I hadn't realized that Louis was ill too. When I read the words "schizoid personality" in reference to Louis, I couldn't believe it. "Not Louis too." My thoughts raced. "I can't go through this again." He had always been a shy, quiet child, so we didn't realize how withdrawn he had become.

At a meeting with the experts, they showed me a sketch that Louis had made during a test. I recognized the sketch immediately as Larry Nivan's puppeteer. Louis was simply making a sketch of something that meant a lot to him, and he was an avid reader of science fiction.

Sam was showing signs of manic-depression, anxiety, and hypochondria.

The school social worker, John Crow, who was a talented man, decided to work with Louis. He had to choose between the two because he could only work with one of them. Louis was the most severely ill.

Mr. Crow did some research. Talking to classmates brought out the shocking story: the two of them were scapegoats, which meant that every child in the school was out to get them and was required not to talk to or be seen socializing with them.

While Mr. Crow was dealing with Louis, I took Sam to a nearby mental health clinic for counseling. Our family agreed to counsel as well. I was not satisfied with the counseling because it seemed to be a waste of time. But we went anyway.

For the next six months, they tried to undo the harm that was done to Sam's ego. One of the symptoms I mentioned before that he had demonstrated was hypochondria, which was focused on his ears. He was afraid that he would lose his hearing. Several trips to the family doctor and an ear specialist could not convince him that his fears were unfounded. It would take five years for Sam to overcome this fear.

While in counseling, the atrocities began to come out. Louis and I unearthed some of the terrible experiences that our boys had had to endure.

We discovered that, for three years, our twins were punched, spit on, and made fun of in a wide and ingenious variety of ways. Among others things, when they got on the school bus in the morning, every day without fail, all the kids would yell, "Boo." When they got off, the crowd would yell, "Yeah." One story I got out of Sam was especially sickening.

"Once while I was taking a shower in school, the boys all started making fun of the size of my penis. They wouldn't stop. One kid took a Polaroid snapshot of me naked and passed it around. It was later posted on the bulletin board where I found it. A note said that copies had been made.

"The story must've gotten around because, the next day, one of the girls in class drew a picture of it on the blackboard, showing how small it was. All the kids cheered and roared. Mom, you don't know how bad that made me feel."

It was a small country school where, as is usual in high schools, all the kids formed cliques. Unknown to Louis and Sam, they had been in the clique with the bright kids. But they were now ostracized from the group by their best friend, who was the group leader. Turk was jealous of Sam because of the high grade he received in biology. Sam and Louis had been belittled over and over.

Both boys found refuge in the school library. The librarian loved them. There in their own little world of books, they escaped for a time the onslaught of terrors that waited for them outside those doors.

Now that he didn't have Louis in his classes, his schoolmates left Sam alone. He also managed to pass most of his courses. But I had to send him to school every day while he was in a depressed state. Some days Samuel would cry continually. It broke my heart to have to do this, although I knew that, if I babied him now, he would never recover.

Because the kids now didn't use Louis as a target, he was able to make new friends.

Mr. Crow came upon the scene during their junior year in high school. To his credit, I have to say he performed his job well because, within the next year, Louis's personality began to change. He had been the sloppy twin, but now he began to develop good grooming habits. Amazingly, he soon began to like himself again.

Once, while eating lunch in the school cafeteria, the school bully unwisely decided to torment Louis. He threw food in his face.

"You do that one more time and you'll be sorry," Louis threatened. He was like his father, strong and tough. And when the thug flung another ball of mashed potatoes at Louis again, his temper turned him into a killing machine. All the fury that had welled up in him because of the abuse he had been taking, let loose.

He punched the boy repeatedly until the bully collapsed on the floor. Only the sight of blood kept him from hammering further with his fist. Two teachers grabbed him but he threw them off. A teacher tried to block his punches, but he fought around the teacher until the kid was down for good.

The fight drew attention from the entire student body because this bully had caused trouble for nearly everyone in the school. Teachers and children alike were disgusted with him.

Finally, it was over, and Louis found himself standing in front of the principal's desk. Because the bully had been such a menace, Louis only got two hours detention for the fight. The bully was suspended.

When Louis returned to his next class, he received a standing ovation from the kids. This time, the cheering was for him. From that day on, Louis was well liked and respected at school.

It wasn't that easy, however, to go from scapegoat to hero. The bully, who was also on probation, sent a message to Louis the next week that his gang was going after him.

"I'll get even," the note said. "My gang will make you wish you were dead."

For the first time in his life, Louis knew real fear. He became so upset that he couldn't study for a test in Algebra III. While Mr. Crow intervened and persuaded the probation board to make the hoodlum leave him alone, he, nevertheless, flunked the test, and subsequently failed the course. It was the first course that Louis had ever failed. After that experience, Louis realized that he couldn't solve all of his problems with his fists.

It would take several years, however, for Sam to develop a healthy ego. His sad experience in school had damaged him emotionally. Besides that, being the more sensitive twin, he always knew that his brother was stronger. He felt inadequate.

When graduation time came near, neither boy would have his picture taken for the school yearbook. They also did not attend the graduation ceremonies. The embarrassed school department had to mail their diplomas to them. Even so, the town voted to give them each a scholarship when they graduated.

That year they were accepted by the University of Rhode Island and began working on their careers. At college, they had to earn their own way by part time jobs on campus and taking advantage of student loans. But college was a better experience for them.

There, they were respected for their knowledge and the grades they earned. Being both highly motivated, they worked hard to attain their goals.

Loius wanted a degree in physics, and Sam, who had always had an interest in human anatomy, wanted his degree in genetics or some related field. For the time being, at least, Louis and Sam were learning how to deal with their genetic predisposition to mental illness.

CHAPTER 13

"Ma, I got the golden key award!" Sam exclaimed over the phone. "And that will get me a job in the lab, doing research."

"On campus?" I queried.

"On campus," my son returned. "It will be part of a work-study program." He caught his breath. "And I get to do tissue culture, something I've always wanted."

Louis and I were proud of both of our sons because they had taken college by storm. Louis was a physics major and was taking the most difficult courses that the university had to offer. Indeed, there were only a few students taking physics because the courses were so difficult, and our son's marks were the highest in the class. Louis was the president of the physics society and was teaching a physics lab at the university. He was doing well.

He had a strong interest in physical fitness and would never miss a workout at the gym. There, he won the competition for the most developed body.

Sam took some of the physics courses during his first two years at college and actually did better than his brother, but he decided early on that genetics was his field of interest.

"Physics is too boring for me. I want more variety. Genetics is more exciting. It's a whole new science," he told me.

It seemed as if we had it all: success, money—yes, even money. We had sold the old house and, with the funds, were in the process of building a new home, a log cabin. It was to be our retirement home. Because the new house would only cost a fraction of the money we had in the bank, Louis and I would invest the remainder and be able to retire. Louis could work on his art full time.

"'Flying high in April, shot down in May.' Isn't that the way the song goes?" I queried to my half sister over the phone. "No one could ever have guessed what was going to happen."

At a time when our future seemed the brightest, Louis was rushed to the hospital with a heart attack. Although he had survived the heart attack, a strange thing happened to him. When I was able to see him in the intensive care unit, he cried. Ribbons of tears rolled down his cheeks, "I'm sorry," he kept on repeating. "I'm sorry I called the boys names."

He told me he had gone to hell, and he was frightened. I told him that if that ever happened again to call upon the name of Jesus Christ. As he cradled my face in his hands and caressed it, he told me he never looked at another woman. Since he had survived the heart attack, we believed he would recover.

I was in the same hospital myself having a major operation, a hysterectomy because I was hemorrhaging. Louis didn't know I was having surgery. I kept it from him because I didn't want him worrying about me. It was the second day after my surgery, and I was ready to visit him by wheelchair. It was a long wait, so I eventually went back to bed.

The nurses kept on telling me that they were having a problem with one of the patients in the intensive care unit. I had no clue that that patient was Louis. But when three doctors and my brother-in-law entered my room and told me that Louis had died, I was shocked with disbelief and in physical pain. I could hardly walk at the funeral. The array of gifts, in the form of food and money, was welcomed, but nothing could replace the man—the husband and father.

The boys were in their senior year at college, and our daughter had just graduated from high school. She was accepted by Rhode

Island College and began her studies in the fall semester. Jonathan, the youngest, was only fifteen, a sophomore in high school. And I had a house to build. Because Louis could not do the carpentry work as we had planned, finishing the house took all of the funds that I had in the bank.

My husband must have known he was dying because he asked all his friends who visited him to help me build the house. Only one friend actually helped me. His name was John Destante. Everyone called him "Big John" because he was almost seven feet tall and weighed over three hundred pounds. Big John was also the mason who was building the fireplace for us. Without his help, the house would never have been built. He knew how to find a plumber, an electrician, and all the other specialists who work on houses.

Carpenters cost a lot of money, I had to admit as I checked my bank statement. With three children in college, I felt lucky that I had a good-paying job in construction. I had graduated from college during a recession, and getting a teacher's job was impossible. But the job in construction paid well. By taking advantage of grants and student loans, none of the children had to quit school.

Each family member had to deal with their loss in their own special way. Although I had a tough constitution, I had nightmares every night for six months. The nightmares were about him going to hell. One nightmare in particular I had was a vision of him coming into my bedroom, grabbing my hand and proceeding to take me to heaven with him. We were both naked.

Halfway up to heaven, he looked down at me, and his face was covered with worms. I woke up screaming. The other dreams were similar in that I always saw Louis cheating on me with another woman. This other woman was very attractive with a gray complexion and long white legs that never seemed to reach the ground. Louis was always trying to communicate with me, but he was not able to do so. I awoke up every morning with feelings of horror and anger at him. I actually was blaming him for dying.

After six months of agony, my father came over for a visit with a book titled The Light Beyond, by Dr. Moody. Through reading this book, I discovered that what Louis had had was a near-death experience. And since he had changed, it meant that he had gone to heaven. Those nightmares disappeared after that realization.

The dreams about the other woman lasted for years though, until I discovered what that dream was trying to tell me. The woman was lady death, and Louis was trying to tell me why he had to leave me. We never had the chance to say goodbye. The dreams have all vanished now, since I finally am at peace with his death.

Life's tragic blows had only made me stronger. My concerns now, along with house building, were to focus on my children, helping them with their struggles.

My daughter Angel began a new phase in her life when she entered college shortly after her father's death. That, along with a new boyfriend, helped to soften the blows for her.

Jonathan, our youngest who was only fifteen when he lost his father, became a man. "I don't feel the sorrow so much, Ma," he told me, "because I got to know my dad in the two years before he died. He was a great guy and I know he's in heaven."

Louis sought counseling at college in order to deal with his father's death. He offered to quit school to support me, but I would not listen to him. "Make your dad proud, Louis, and continue your studies." He was always a slugger like Louis, so now he threw himself into his career.

Sam suffered the most. He had never gotten along well with his father and now felt the full force of his loss. Feelings of guilt and emotional pain caused problems in school, as his marks began to plummet. The hypochondria returned, and he spent many hours in the health services department at the university.

He complained of many physical problems which, for the most part, didn't exist. The first semester after the funeral, he took incomplete grades in all of his courses. "I just can't seem to study, Ma," he explained to me.

He also complained of girl problems. His sexual drive was heightened so much so that, seeing a pretty girl walk by would send him into depression. He never had the courage to talk to girls. The next semester he got low marks and was taken off the dean's list.

Bellyaching about everything, he no longer believed in God and had such a negative outlook on life that no one could stand to have him around.

"He's pulling me down, Mom," Louis confided to me. Louis, who had been his roommate in college for four years, was now ashamed of his brother.

"If I let him bother me, I'll start to flunk myself."

"Just take care of yourself, Louis," I advised my son. "Pray for him."

I knew that Sam was going through emotional turmoil. I had been there myself. Yet I didn't know how to help him. He had requested counseling at school, but no one seemed to care. They all told him that he was normal.

When the twins came home for Thanksgiving break, Sam looked so terrible that I was even more alarmed. He had lost a great deal of weight and was desperately unhappy. I feared that he was having a nervous breakdown. Frantically, I called psychiatrists and counselors, including Mr. Crow who agreed to see him. But Sam refused all help.

"I have to do this myself, Mom. I want to be a man. I can't always rely on you."

Then the inevitable happened. During final exams, Sam was rushed to Fuller Memorial Hospital in Attleboro, a mental hospital. He signed himself in. I got the call while I was at work. I had been working sixty-four hours a week because I desperately needed the money. And now this crushing news.

"Stone eyes. That's what they call it, Ma," Sam told me when he saw my reaction to his gaze. I had gone to visit him at Fuller's. "My eyes are reacting to the medication."

He had the same look in his eyes that lion in my nightmares had. Now I knew that the lion must've been a symbol of my brother Sam. I feared to look in his eyes. It was the same dilated look that my son had. I had to face the anguish again. My heart seemed to stop; as I felt the pain, the same pain I had to face as a child, only this time I couldn't escape it. This time there was no running away from it. This time I had to tackle the demon head on. My own son was mentally ill.

Sam could best tell the story in his own words: "I had diarrhea, severe bellyaches, and headaches, and I thought I had some sort of tropical disease. Finally I went to see the psychiatrist at school. I had been running around for days, not knowing what to do.

"Dr. Feldman from the university decided that I should be admitted to the hospital. He said that he thinks I'm having an anxiety attack. I needed immediate attention.

"I was sure I had a physical disease and that they would find out what it was in the hospital. But they tested me for a variety of things, including diabetes and a thyroid condition. They found nothing wrong.

"It was all in my head. My heart was pounding at twice the speed as is normal, and my blood pressure was very high. The bellyaches—all of it, I was doing it to myself.

"I talked to my doctor in the hospital, Dr. Boyd, who helped me tremendously. I was so depressed that, at first, she thought I was manic-depressive. But she ruled that out because my mood fluctuations were so rapid. A manic depressive usually stays depressed for months."

Al seemed to be feeling better that day but the next day, when I went to visit him again, he was in such a deep depression that his eyes were half closed. The day before, in his anxious state, he literally did cartwheels in the hallway. Now they had him in the "quiet room" where he was trying to sleep.

"Here, you take it," he said as he handed me the tip of a ballpoint pen. "I was going to use it to puncture my jugular vein and kill myself. But I decided to fight it. If I'm intelligent enough to find a way to kill myself in an institution, then I'm smart enough to find a way out of this.

"After I found out I had no physical problems, I started to believe that I was going crazy. I tried to read and couldn't make sense of the words.

"Then this crazy woman in the room next to mine kept on flushing the toilet. She couldn't stop. I couldn't stand it. That's when I had the fit and contemplated suicide."

The amazing thing, to me at least, was that his personality changed so quickly. After all those years of negative thinking—all that suffering, here he was standing before me a changed person.

For the first time in his life, he was thinking positively. He was a Christian again. What's more, he now liked himself. He recovered from his anxiety attack in a week and a half and was released shortly afterward.

"How did this happen?" I wanted to know a few days later. I was hoping that this transformation was a permanent part of his personality.

"Mom, it happened right after I gave you the pen tip. I prayed. I said to God, 'All right, so I'm going to spend the rest of my life as a crazy person. That's okay. But I'm going to fight it every step of the way.'

"Then a miracle happened. I guess you could call it a miracle. I started to respect myself for the first time in my life. I have always thought of myself as a coward and have hated myself for it; now I realize how brave I am. If I could face something as bad as going crazy and still decide to fight, then I must have a lot of courage. Mom, I'm a great guy.

"I also told God that, 'If you let me read again, I'll read your Bible.' And you know what? I picked up a book and read it. I could read. I can understand the words. Again."

In the weeks that followed I watched my son closely for signs of a relapse. But none came. Not yet anyway. I believed that my son was cured. He went back to college to finish his last semester.

Four months later, he returned home to face unemployment lines. We were in the middle of a recession. He got a temporary job in his field for five months. But when the job was finished, he found himself out of work again. Undaunted by that, he looked aggressively for work again. Finally, he found a permanent job in a lab testing oils for foods. All looked well. Two weeks after getting the job, Sam came home one morning.

"Why are you home so early?" I asked.

"Mom, they called me into the front office today. They sent a policeman to get me. When I got there, they told me my employment was terminated. When I asked why, they told me it was because of my medication. Part of my job was to get an oil sample from one of the tank trucks that come into the yard. They were afraid that, when I climbed the tank to collect the sample I'd get dizzy.

"Mom, that's ridiculous. You know I never get dizzy. They were afraid I'd fall and sue the company. The policeman escorted me out the door. I felt like a common criminal. I almost wish I had lied when I took the physical. But don't worry, Mom. I'll find another job."

In the weeks that followed, Sam tried to remain positive. But with no job prospects and no unemployment checks, he was getting more and more depressed.

One day, in the middle of a winter snowstorm, Sam and I heard the sounds of sirens. They were getting closer and closer. The sound stopped suddenly in front of our house. When we looked out the window, we saw smoke bellowing out of our neighbor's barn. Then we watched in horror as the firemen tried to set up their hoses.

The floor on which we were standing grew uncomfortably hot and we decided to get out of the house. Flames were coming out of the barn and sparks were flying all over the place. A lot of sparks were landing on the roof of our house, and but for the snowstorm, I believe we would have lost our home. Sam took the important papers and few family possessions out on the front porch. Would our house be next?

We were standing on the porch when we heard the telephone ring. Sam went inside and answered it. Several minutes later he bounded outside.

"Ma, it's Louis," he shouted. "He's barricaded up the door to his room, and he's threatening suicide."

Louis had graduated from college and was working on his master's degree. He had a stipend and was a teacher assistant. We had thought he was doing well. He was renting a house with two roommates, one mile from college.

It began to snow heavier but it didn't hamper the fire. It had burst through the roof of the barn with a vengeance, and sparks were flying in all directions. But the fire was of second importance. Now.

Sam got down on his knees. "Pray with me, Mom," he said. "Pray that Louis won't do anything until we get there."

The two of us sent an urgent message to God and then got into the family car. We faced the snowstorm that was raging outside.

I insisted on driving. I felt that my years of driving experience made me more capable. We slid and skidded for half of the fifty-mile trip. The roads hadn't been plowed yet, and the announcer on the radio kept warning people to stay off the roads.

"Only go out if it's absolutely necessary," the announcer kept broadcasting.

But Sam and I prayed our way through the white blanket of snow that seemed to engulf us.

"Oh, dear God, make Louis be all right," we pleaded.

CHAPTER 14

We saw flashing lights in the distance. Could it be? Yes, it was a snowplow. We could see its black silhouette outlined in the middle of the whiteness that surrounded us. Safe at last. I hugged close to the wake of the truck, feeling the sand gripping beneath the tires.

I drove this way for what seemed forever, until I saw the intersection where Louis lived. We were almost there. A few more slips and turns and we could see Louis's white cottage. There was an eerie silence when we got out of the car. Sam burst into the house.

"Where's Louis?" he demanded.

"He's still in his room," his frightened roommates managed to stutter.

Sam gingerly knocked on the door. "Are you all right? Louis? Louis?"

The faint voice that answered didn't sound like his brother. "Sam, I think I'm dying from AIDS."

"AIDS! Louis, you're out of your mind. You're a virgin. You've never done anything to come into contact with AIDS," Sam told him.

But Sam and I knew the truth. Louis too was succumbing to mental illness. He had held out for a long time. He was strong like a bull. He had never backed down from a fight. He would plow into his studies. He was tough, a determined man. But the illness finally got the better of him.

Sam and I stayed with him all night and were reluctant to leave him in the morning. But Louis was feeling better now and was determined to get back to work. Sam and I returned home the following day, even though we knew full well that his brother and my son would soon be in a hospital.

As we rode by the still smoldering barn, it reminded me of my life at that time. Our house was intact, but I owed a pile of bills. Also, two of my children had been struck by the disease that had killed my brother and crippled my sister.

The following week Louis went out of his mind. He ran down the street, banging on each door as he passed. At one house, a black man let him in. Louis begged to be taken to Fuller, the same hospital that Sam had been rushed to two years earlier. The black man called the rescue squad.

At the hospital, Louis was diagnosed with anxiety disease as well, but two doctors conferred he was also suffering with hypochondria. This led him to have a fixation with AIDS. He had never had sexual intercourse nor taken IV Drugs. His AIDS fixation was all in his head.

After a week in the hospital, he returned to work. Although he was on medication, he couldn't perform his job effectively. He quit as conscientiously as he could by finishing the semester teaching and taking incomplete marks in all but one of his courses. Then he came home to live. He had no car, so I took him every week to an outpatient clinic where doctors treated him for his AIDS problem by an experimental drug called Anafranil.

I had had to support three children. Louis was too ill to work, and Sam's depression grew worse each year. Jonathan was a senior in high school. I could never have lived through the ordeal without becoming ill myself if I hadn't had a strong faith in God.

The corners of Sam's mouth bent down in a constant grimace, and I could tell by looking in his eyes that he was very unhappy.

He began to torture me. It was mental torture, but it was torture nevertheless.

"Ma," he would say, "you're the cause of all my problems. You and Dad. You shouldn't have had any children."

He swore at me and called me terrible names, and Louis chimed in. "You and your born-again Christians. You told me I'd go to hell if I didn't believe in God. You know I'm a scientist. And scientists have to see something in order to believe. Where's God now? Why don't I have a job? I curse God. I don't need him; I can do it without him."

One day, while I was at work, Sam got a hold of some nightsticks he found in the cellar and began to make big round holes in the walls. Then he attacked the cellar door.

When I came home from work that day, Louis told me. "Ma, Sam smashed the door but he tried to fix it again. See, it doesn't look too bad now. You should have seen it before."

I had a sinking feeling inside me. I remembered the violence when I was a child. "It's happening again," I thought. How could I bear it?

I let the incident go by without comment, only feeling sick inside. The next day, when I came home from a grueling day at work, Louis met me on the front porch. I knew something terrible had happened.

"Where's Sam?" I asked.

"I kicked him out of the house," he told me. "I didn't like the way he was treating you. Ma, don't go inside. You won't like it."

But I couldn't wait to check out the problem, even though I dreaded going inside. As I climbed the stairs to the side door, I saw that the television set had been thrown over the railing of the porch. It was broken into little pieces. It lay on the ground in shambles, a symbol of what our lives had become.

"What happened? Who did this?" I said angrily.

"I smashed it with the chair. I had to do something to make Sam leave. It was either that or I was going to kill him."

I saw red. The room was spinning around. Then I burst into violence.

"Get out!" I screamed at my son. "You too. And don't come back. Ever. I can't take it anymore."

Loius had expected this. In less than ten minutes he left with a backpack slung over his shoulders. The ground was covered with snow, and I knew he had no money.

I stood alone in the house and watched him disappear around the mailbox. My two sons. My twins. How I loved them. "O, God," I cried. "Please help me," I prayed, as tears clung to my eyes.

I felt loneliness creep in. I was shocked by the violence in my children. Why, they were like my father, and for the first time in my life I began to understand my father and even began to love him more. He must've had anxiety disease or even manic-depression. I remembered watching his hands tremble when I was a young girl. I knew my sons were in anguish. My father must've experienced the pain too.

That night, when I was undressing for bed, I saw bumps on my body. I recognized that they were hives. I had had hives before. They were probably caused by stress.

My youngest son Jonathan was a source of strength to me that night. He comforted me in my anguish. I knew I had to be firm with my sons, but I didn't want to hurt them. It was bitter cold outside. I called my best friend and found out, as I had suspected, that Sam was staying with her.

"Don't tell Sam I called," I told my friend Anita. I told her what had happened. Sam needed to find himself, and he had to get away from his mother.

Later on that night, I got a collect call from Louis. "I'm in Providence," he said. "I'm going to get a ride back home and kill myself in front of my family. Nobody cares for me and I don't care either."

After he hung up, I called the police and told them to find Louis and take him to a hospital. "He's sick," I said. "Please, find him and take him to a hospital."

Then I spent the entire night on the telephone, trying to locate Louis. Because of patient confidentiality, the hospitals wouldn't give out the information. Finally, because I pleaded with them, they did let me know that he was safe.

The police had taken Louis to Butler's Hospital, a mental hospital in Rhode Island where he was diagnosed as being manic-depressive. It was in November, and it was the second time that Louis had been hospitalized in November. Maybe this was a coincidence, but I took a mental note of it.

I decided to let him stay there during Thanksgiving, to teach him a lesson. But Sam didn't want his brother to have his Thanksgiving dinner in a hospital, so he took him out on a day pass to eat with him.

My youngest son and I spent Thanksgiving Day alone. The following day, Louis called from the hospital and asked if he could come home.

"Yes, you may, Louis," I told him, "as long as you don't break anything."

"I won't, Ma, they're giving me medication to help with my mood swings."

The doctor explained later to me that he was taking lithium to help control his moods. Louis came home a week later. He was heavily sedated and depressed most of the time. He threatened suicide many times and kept calling his minister for counseling. He still believed he had AIDS and was convinced that he was dying.

When he became manic, he displayed violent temper tantrums. Once, he threw a full mayonnaise jar across the kitchen, and another time he took his anger out on his photograph that hung on my picture wall. I lived in fear of him, and friends were afraid to visit us.

Two weeks after Sam moved in with Anita, he answered an ad in the newspaper. After an interview, he got the job working as a water tester and moved into an apartment in his boss's condominium on the beach in Newport, Rhode Island. He was losing weight fast and looked miserably unhappy. For three months, he lost all contact with me, except when he came home often to take Louis out to spend the day with him.

In the weeks that followed Louis remained depressed, and when I got a glimpse of Sam on one rare occasion, I knew he was deeply troubled.

His boss was exploiting him. He was giving Sam only $50 for a sixty-hour workweek. Sam expected no forgiveness, and one night, when he was talking to me, he was surprised that I offered him opportunity to come home again. He jumped at the chance, and within a week, he had moved into the basement.

"You can stay with me as long you don't cause any trouble or break things. If you do, out you go," I told him.

Sam understood.

When Louis was in his depression phase, he would stay in bed most of the time, threatening to kill himself. "I know I'm going to die. I know I have AIDS. Curse you God and Jesus Christ for making this happen to me. Why did you give me AIDS? I hate you "

Sometimes he was against God, and other times he would turn to God for comfort. He called the pastor of our church often.

"Please help me," he would scream. "Why does God hate me? I'm sorry for my sins. Please make the devil go away."

Once he made the pastor and his mother exorcise him and cast the devil out of him.

"He's making me curse," he would say.

As bad as Louis's depression was, when he was in mania, he would be worse. He became very violent, and everyone was afraid to live with him. He would threaten to kill people in a variety of ways. He knew how to do this because he was bright and very dangerous.

I prayed hard and clung to my sanity with all my might.

This continued for a year. In the meantime, Sam found a good job working in a laboratory. He was doing some of the things he only dreamed of doing when he was a child. He was highly motivated and very happy. It was only a temporary job, But Sam was hoping the company would eventually make him a full-time employee.

In order to maintain his separation from his brother and his mother, he built himself an apartment in the basement. Although he didn't have enough money to board the walls and the ceiling up, he nevertheless built himself a wall out of leftover logs. He built the revolving wall out of scraps of logs he found in the cellar.

He built the wall five-inch thick with pine boards from the floor, which pivoted around a one-and-a-half-inch pipe. He drilled the pipe into the cellar floor. It was an ingenious invention, and it served the purpose he had in mind. When the wall was closed, it looked and fulfilled its purpose of being simply a wall. No one could tell it was anything other than a wall. When he swung it around, it served as a door.

In this manner Sam maintained his privacy. Louis and I only came in when we were invited.

November became the month I dreaded, and November in '92 was worse than I had ever imagined it could be. My youngest son Jonathan was now a sophomore at the university studying microbiology like his brother Sam. His personality was entirely different from his older brothers.

To begin with, unlike his muscular brother, Jonathan was small in stature. He also was my most honest child. He was so sincere and so honest that it made him easy prey for some evangelists who told him he was going to hell if he didn't get baptized. He came home from college one weekend in a state of anxiety.

"Mom," he asked me. "Do you think I'm going to hell?"

I assured him that was not the way I interpreted the Bible, and after all, I had studied the Bible for years.

All my explanations did no good. Jonathan returned to college and was rushed to Butler Hospital in a state of mania one week later. When I went to see him in the hospital, his eyes were half closed. While there, his psychiatrist told him to stay away from religion until he was well enough to handle it. Jonathan had to drop out of college temporarily while his mind had a chance to mend.

In the meantime, Louis had called the Mental Health Clinic in Jackson, Rhode Island, where he was then being treated, and told them he wanted them to get him a job. And because he had threatened them before, saying that he would use a gun against them, they called the police. Four policemen came to the house and handcuffed him and took him away in a cruiser. One caring officer came into the house and informed me and Sam they would take him to a hospital. He would have no police record. Louis was taken to St. Joseph's Hospital in Providence.

After a week in the hospital, Jonathan and Louis came home again to live with me. Jonathan recovered quickly and went to work as a landscaper.

I was relieved for Jonathan when he told me that he was moving in with some college friends.

"I'll never get well living here," he told me, and I knew this was a wise decision. I had to trust one son to God.

If it wasn't for those three little pills I took each night to make me sleep, I don't believe I could have been able to go on. That, along with my strong faith in God, kept me sane. The hives covered my entire body, even my head. The itching would keep me from sleeping on occasion.

I went to Roger Williams Hospital for treatment, but all the doctors could do was to give me some pills to stop the itch. I had a huge welt that covered my entire neck, and when I went to bed, I had to use a silk scarf which I placed across my neck in order to get to sleep. It prevented me from scratching.

Then, to make matters worse, my face began to swell up. One side of my mouth swelled up first. The following day, it would be the other side of my mouth. Then my eyes took turns swelling up. This went on for a year and a half. Then one day, they miraculously disappeared. The only reminder I had that I ever had the hives at all was a small bag under my left eye.

The only other thing I had going for me was my job. Because I worked in traffic all day, my mind would have to concentrate entirely on what was going on at work.

I rarely saw my mother and sister or the rest of the family because I was too busy, and I had problems that I preferred not to discuss with others about.

I did not know what was happening to my children because I didn't know much about mental illness. I decided it was about time I found out, so I began to get my hands on all the information I could about this monster so I could tackle him head on.

CHAPTER 15

In 1997 I began to consult many books about mental illness in order to find out what was happening to my family. What I found out was that ten percent of the American people are suffering from or will suffer from some sort of mental illness in their lifetimes.

Among these, more than two million are burdened by schizophrenia. And for each of those persons, there is a family that will be greatly affected by the devastating effects of this disease. Today we are finding out that there are a lot more cases of reported mental illness. Therefore, taking the families into account, most of us will have some contact with mental illness in the course of our lives. That means that what was happening to my family was not that unusual.

It was not too long ago when the insane were chained to walls in dungeons. In the not-to-recent history, experimental drugs and various other treatments like electric shock therapy were used to treat the mentally ill. I am pleased to report that electric shock treatment has improved drastically through the years, and many other drugs are on the market today.

Frustrated doctors tried in vain one drug after another, with little or no success in order to treat this malady. Even today, not enough is understood about the disease. But for the most part, thanks to science and the tireless efforts of dedicated professionals, most mental patients can and do lead normal, productive lives.

So many books have been written on mental illness, and so many different types of professions have been established to treat it that, to the lay person, this disease remains a mystery. Furthermore, the media hasn't helped to curb the growing misunderstanding— the stigma—that is associated with this disease.

To alleviate some of the misconceptions, this chapter is an attempt to explain, in simple language, the different types of mental illness, the causes, and what is being done at present to treat them.

> Mental illness falls into two major categories: psychosis and neurosis, and the use of even these terms today is frowned upon by psychiatrists and psychologists. In neurosis, the patient usually has a mild to moderate impairment of personal and social functioning; in psychosis their impairment is severe.[1]

Psychosis

A person who has psychosis fails to distinguish between his fantasies and the facts of his case. In other words, he doesn't have a firm grip on reality. Now I could understand more clearly what was going on with my children. Their illness was something they couldn't control.

The National Classification of Diseases in 1955 lists eight specific psychoses. Four of these, called organic psychoses (senile, pre-senile, arteriosclerosis, alcoholic) are the result of degenerative changes in the brain or brain damage. Also, they usually occur later on in life. For that reason, I won't cover them here.

The other four (functional psychoses), schizophrenia, manic-depression, involutional melancholia, and paranoia, are of great interest to me because they usually develop early in life. I was to

---

[1]   J. Colemand, Abnormal Psychology and Modern Life

hear these terms many times during the course of my family's illnesses.

1. Schizophrenia

The most feared psychosis and the worst of all is common to one percent of the population, and usually has its inception in adolescence, although it sometimes may be developed in early childhood. The term schizophrenia means "split mind," and was coined by Eugene Bleuler, the medical director at Holzi Hospital in Zurich. He believed that in this disease, there is a splitting or loss of coordination between different psychic functions -the intellectual and the emotional.

> Schizophrenia is recognized as the most important single cause of chronic psychiatric disabilities. In this disease the subject loses control of his will and he hears voices telling him what to do. Withdrawal is considered to be the central phenomenon of the schizophrenic process.
> The patient retreats into fantasy. His feelings take shape as delusions and hallucinations and other phantoms. If his isolation becomes chronic, the fabric of his entire life begins to unravel. He forgets how to be a person in a particular society. As he drifts away from everyone else he becomes set in his own eccentric ways.[2]

In time, Louis displayed symptoms of this disease. Every night before I went to bed, he told me that I would not wake up in the morning because he was going to kill me in my sleep. I became very frightened each time it happened, but God was with us. Each time that happened, I would tell him he'd have to leave. One night, he spent the entire night packing. Also, Louis folded up every bit of his belongings very carefully.

---

[2] Gregory, *Oxford Companion to the Mind*

The next morning, he cried, put his arms around me, and said, "Mom, I would never, ever hurt you. It's just these voices in my head telling me what to do."

Each morning, I would forgive him and would spend the entire day in constant prayer.

I discovered through my reading that there is no doubt that this disease is, at least in part, transmitted genetically. There is also no doubt that environmental factors are important. The twins' horrific experience in high school was no doubt the trigger that caused this monster to raise its horrible head.

I was taken completely by surprise when the fiend showed up in my family. My brother Jack had five normal children. I fully expected mine to be normal too. I asked myself over and over what made the difference. Why should my children be affected by this disease?

The common denominator had to be Bob. Louis suffered from depression. Also, I had been ill myself. My poor children inherited bad genes from both their father and their mother.

Also, why should my brother Sam have become ill as well as my sister? The insanity must've come from both my mother and my father. Almost every one of my aunts and uncles on my mother's side of the family had some form of mental illness. However, all of the 108 cousins on my mother's side were normal. The four of my mother's children became ill because my father was an alcoholic. We got a double dose of the bad genes.

My brother Jack never showed the illness yet he, like father, needed alcohol on a daily basis.

The good news is that since the middle of the 1950s, tranquilizers and other drugs are used to control the acute illness and reduce the risk of relapse, and scientists today are working with unfailing enthusiasm to develop new medication and learn how to 'weed out the gene" in the genetic code that causes this disease.

Furthermore, it also was found that patients actually got worse in hospitals.

Because of the use of these drugs, and because of a change in public and psychiatric policies, the evils of institutionalization are avoided, and many schizophrenics, who in the past would have had to spend forty or fifty years in an asylum, are now able to live useful and even happy lives. Approximately 1/3 recover, 1/3 partially recover, and 1/3 are disabled (usually living in halfway houses)"[3]

2. Manic-depression

Also called bipolar because the emotional part of the person is affected rather than his thought processes. A personality oscillating between overactivity and the inability to summon up energy to make decisions is considered manic-depressive.

In his depressed state, the person usually stays in bed or walks in a hunched position. He feels tired constantly. He may lie in one position for hours. That's why Louis stayed in bed for days. Other depressed patients become restless.

They may pace or wring their hands. They act as if they are facing a terrible calamity. The person in his manic stage becomes angry every time he is contradicted and every time his wishes are frustrated. While in his manic state, a person may be very creative.

The causes for manic depression are the same for schizophrenia: a predisposition caused by genetics and an unhealthy environment.

Many manic-depressive personalities do very well in society while using the drug lithium, tranquilizers, and anti-anxiety drugs, although they may have several episodes, which may require hospitalization from time to time. If they stop taking their medicine, however, their chances of becoming psychotic again are eight to ten times greater than they would have been otherwise.

---

[3]   Ibid.

3. Melancholia

Melancholia is a severe depression appearing without manic attacks. This person may have difficulty sleeping and eating. He may lose weight and even try to commit suicide. This is not to be confused with depression, a neurosis.

The causes of this illness are the same as manic-depression.

Lithium and Prozac have been used with some success. Also, electric shock treatment may cure this disease.

4. Paranoia

> Paranoia is the name given to one type of functional psychosis that in which the patient holds a belief centering around the conviction that he (or sometimes she) is a person of great importance and is on that account being persecuted, despised, and rejected. True paranoia is, fortunately, rare.[4]

There are no known causes at present. However, the family background seems to be dominating and critical to excess. He needs to prove that he is superior.

It has no known treatment or cure. However, as in the case of my Uncle Henry, a person can live a useful and even happy life while living with this disease.

Neurosis

Neurosis, the most common form of mental illness, is a fixed habit. This habit is usually distressing and greatly affects normal living.

---

4   Ibid.

1. Obsessions/compulsions

> An obsessive personality is one who is conventionally conscientious, reliably scrupulous, or punctual well beyond average. These characteristics could be essential qualities for anyone engaged in precision work as in scientific research. But in comparison, anyone who suffers from an obsession/compulsion is sick.[5]

We used to tease Louis about being scrupulous about his habits. For instance, he used to (and still does) line up his shoes in a particular pattern. He even used to line up the shoelaces! We did not know that it was a neurosis.

> This neuroses is rare, affecting only .05% of the population, but 12-20% of the neurotic population. The symptoms that an obsessive/compulsive can have can cripple the performance of everyday activities, as resisting the compulsion can arouse acute distress.
>
> This person shows a very strong fear of being contaminated, of coming into contact with germs, dirt, or other substances. He cleans and washes himself constantly to reduce his fears. This cleaning/washing behavior gradually can increase in frequency and becomes so obsessive that it takes up practically all of his waking hours.[6]

The cause for this illness can be attributed to superstitious thoughts. Thank God, Louis's obsessions do not interfere with his work.

A disorder of this kind is obviously very serious, but thanks to a treatment called response prevention, psychologists can cure

---

[5] Eysenck, Mind Watching, Why People Behave the Way They Do
[6] Ibid.

the person without medication by some form of reeducation or reconditioning.

Here's how it's done briefly: After the patient has been explained the details of the treatment, and when the psychologist obtains his informed consent, he is brought into a room which contains little else beside a table, two chairs, and a container filled with some dirt or other material that the person is known to think of as "contaminating." The patient is then persuaded to put his hand into the dirt and not to wash his hands. He is then asked to endure the very strong emotions of fear, anguish, and anxiety that threaten to overwhelm him.

By this relearning process, the patient gradually recovers. The treatment works, and works well in almost all of the cases, and it does so in fewer than twenty supervised exposures.

Loius has found a way out of his "AIDS" problem. He periodically goes in for an AIDS test.

2. Phobias

Phobic persons fall into two main groups: (1) Those who have a fear of a specified set such as a dog, etc. These people show no other symptoms, and (2) those who exhibit unusually intense fear in a number of situations. The latter are the most sick, are usually reluctant to leave home, and are described as agoraphobic.

The theory holds that when a person is intensely afraid of something that others do not fear, it is because the object or situation in question has become associated in his mind with a childhood fear, as of loud noises or falling (this could explain Marla's fear of the thunder). The other theory believes that the feared object or situation has become symbolic of something feared unconsciously (my phobia).

> The specific or limited phobias are cured by means of desensitization.
> Sensitization is a state in which nerves are conditioned to react to stress in an exaggerated way; they bring unusually

intense feelings when under stress and at times with alarming swiftness.

Severe sensitization can cause the following symptoms: rapid heartbeat, palpitations, upset stomach, shaking hands, sweating, inability to breathe deeply, difficulty swallowing, feelings of weakness, headaches, or giddiness. The habit of fear must be cured. There are four simple rules to cure phobias.

Face: do not run away.
Accept: do not fight.
Float pass: do not arrest and listen in.
Let time pass: do not be impatient with time.[7]

Reading many books on the subject, and also sessions with a psychologist will usually bring about a cure.

3. Hypochondriac neurosis

The individual is preoccupied with his state of health and with various disorders or diseases of bodily organs. Samuel suffers with this a great deal.

The cause may be an overemphasis on bodily functions in early life, sometimes an early childhood illness in which the child has received a lot of attention. Samuel was always seeking attention from me, and I did not realize that my constant attention was feeding his illness.

The cure for this is, after a competent doctor's diagnosis that there is nothing wrong with the patient physically, ignore his symptoms. Force him to take part in his activities (school, etc.).

---

[7]   Dr. Claire Weekes, *Peace from Nervous Suffering*

4. Anxiety disease

"Anxiety neuroses involve mental and physical symptoms caused by the abnormal fear or dread of death or insanity or other conditions that could disable the individual. I have recently been involved in an accident in which I completely totaled my car.

Now, I have a dreadful fear of driving, even if someone else is doing the driving. I'm scared to death whenever I get in an automobile. My anxiety is so bad that I have to take medicine for it. However, I know that I can't let this thing beat me. If I let it, it could cripple me to the point that I remain at home and become a slave to my illness. To counter this anxiety, I force myself to drive somewhere every day. It's not easy, but the alternative would be far worse.

> There are two kinds of anxiety: exogenous and endogenous. Exogenous anxiety is a normal reaction to stress outside the individual. This type is experienced by everyone and is caused by a justifiable sense of fear, which comes from outside of the person, such as a dangerous animal, etc.
> The second type or endogenous anxiety is a disease whose victims appear to be born with, a genetic vulnerability for. It usually starts with spasms of anxiety that appear without warning. The heart may race, the person experiences lightheadedness, faintness or dizzy spells, imbalance, and jelly legs. He may have chest pain, or pressure, a choking sensation, a tingling sensation or numbness in parts of his body, nausea, hot flashes, diarrhea, headaches, obsessions, and compulsions. Sixty percent of these victims also complain that they feel that things around them become strange, unreal, foggy, or detached.[8]

---

[8]   Sheenan, The Anxiety Disease

This is the disease that Samuel has. Without his medication, he would suffer tremendously.

The causes of anxiety disease are three fold: biological, psychological, and conditioning and stress. It seems to be inherited. Just as Pavlov's dogs learned to associate bells with food, the person with this disease can be conditioned to have a reaction. For instance, if he first experiences anxiety while he was riding in an elevator, he will probably have recurrent reactions whenever he finds himself in the elevator again.

A person with anxiety disease usually has many phobias. Like ripples in a pond, phobias and anxiety spread in a similar way. Many parents who have children with this disease blame themselves. However, studies show that it is not caused by childhood rearing practices.

If you find out that your son (or daughter) has anxiety disease, you should get a diagnosis from a reliable psychiatrist. The diagnosis is only a tool that doctors use in determining this malady. The doctor then prescribes the appropriate medicine. It may take years to obtain the correct medicine because medicines react in different ways for different patients.

A word of caution: the diagnosis can change. For instance, Samuel's initial diagnosis was anxiety disorder. Later on, when he was hospitalized again, it became manic-depression. Marla had a number of diagnoses. At first they said she was having seizures, then schizophrenia. Both diagnoses were wrong.

After diagnoses from a competent psychiatrist, your child may have to learn to deal with psychological problems through sessions with a trained psychologist.

5. Traumatic shock

This is the neurosis which I had when I was twenty-eight years old. It is an overwhelming emotional experience that causes the disruption of mental and physical functions or behavior.

The first stage is a rage which usually is of very short duration. This is followed by severe depression. The physical complications that are usually manifested are loss of sleep, poor appetite, and disorientation, leading to exhaustion and disability.

This illness is commonly caused by the loss of a loved one. Usually the patient is treated with tranquilizers and/or sleeping pills, and rest. In severe cases, hospitalization may be required.

6. Depression

> A severe emotional disturbance. There are two types of depression: (1) Reactive or neurotic depression is an understandable response in a vulnerable personality to lesser or greater degrees of misfortunes, bereavement, financial loss, illness, etc. (2) Endogenous depression is when a sufferer will manifest a state of deep despondency and hopelessness coupled in some instances with self-accusations and guilt over trivial matters.
> There may be evidence for a genetic predisposition to this disease.
> Note: All persons with depression should be assessed for the risk of suicide. All mention of suicide by a depressed person must be taken with the utmost seriousness so that immediate admission to a hospital can be arranged if necessary.[9]

Depression is usually cured with antidepressants and sometimes with counseling by a psychologist. Electric shock therapy has been used to cure depression.

7. Conversion hysteria

This is commonly called nervous collapse. It causes physical symptoms such as paralysis, numbness, or even convulsions. This is probably what I had after my stepfather tried to kill my mother and me.

---

[9]   Gregory, Oxford Companion to the Mind

It is usually preceded by periods of extreme stress or exhaustion.

The cure is treatment with tranquilizers and rest.

Note: These are general descriptions of mental illness. However, there are no set rules of symptoms in this disease. Most mental patients display the symptoms of more than one illness. For example, Louis suffered from manic-depression and anxiety disease with hypochondriac tendencies. Samuel was manic-depressive also, but he mostly had the symptoms of anxiety disease.

It all was beginning to make sense to me now. By understanding what my children were experiencing and that there were professionals to talk to about our family "curse" (which was what we called it), it allowed me to see that there was some sort of future for my children. Their lives had been difficult, but happiness for them was possible.

The following terms will also be of interest to you.

Nervous breakdown

A break with reality is commonly called a nervous breakdown. This term has no meaning in medicine, and doctors do not use it. Laymen often use the term to describe any nervous behavioral disturbance that takes part in a previously healthy person, which requires him to be hospitalized.

Insanity

Insanity is a legal term, which refers to any type of mental illness that requires a court to commit a person into a hospital or appoint a legal guardian for him.

Tic

A tic is a habitual spasmodic contraction of certain muscles, especially of the face.

Psychopathic personality

Strictly speaking, this term should be applied to all varieties of abnormal persons who make the community suffer because of it. The Mental Health Act of 1959 defined psychopathic disorder as a "persistent disorder or disability of mind (whether or not including sub-normality of intelligence) which results in abnormally aggressive or seriously irresponsible conduct on the part of the patient, and requires or is susceptible to medical treatment." In the Mental Health Act of 1983, however, the last seven words of this definition are omitted.

The term is used mainly because it is important to make a distinction between the mentally healthy offender and the presumably mentally abnormal one. Also, it was widely believed that this form of insanity was responsible for the actions of individuals who exhibited a persistent tendency to indulge in criminal behavior. Also, many psychiatrists would have reservations about claims that psychopathic personality is a mental illness on a par with neurosis or psychosis.

Theories as to its cause have included brain damage in childhood, late maturation of the central nervous system, and adverse circumstances of upbringing, particularly difficult relationships with parents and those in authority.

Because the psychopath appears to lack the inner controls normally developed during childhood and adolescence, it is believed that sympathetic handling in a disciplined environment brings some results. I believe that a psychopath is a person who has no conscience, and that is the difference between him and my three sons.

Note: From the adverse exposure given by the media, most people fear any sign of and anyone having a connection to mental illness. The facts, however, show that most people who are mentally ill are not dangerous but kind, caring, and sensitive people, some of the best people in the world.

Whatever the type of mental illness, a happy, healthy environment goes a long way in preventing its inception.

CHAPTER 16

I began to ask more questions. What about my family? Four children, each born to the same parents, the same mother and father, the same bloodlines. Why did two become hopelessly mentally ill, while the others did not? All of us had inherited the tendency to mental illness. Marla never held a job, never married, never had children, never traveled, in short, never accomplished anything. And I had a successful life. Why? And why didn't Jack Junior become ill when his older brother died in a mental institution?

There are many answers to these questions, each as diverse in its own way. And all of them give the answer to a part of the story.

In the first place, no two people are alike. Each case of mental illness is different, and each person leads his life in his own particular way. Although circumstances may be the same for two people, their reactions to the same circumstances can be different.

There were four children in the Midsummer family, and each occupied his/her own special place in the group. The position that a person has in the family group can determine, in part, how a particular child will react to situations. And how he is treated by his parents.

Studies have shown that the oldest child and the youngest child are more at risk of having emotional problems than the other siblings. Parents treat their firstborn differently than they treat the rest of their children. When the first child is born, they lack experience in child rearing. For that reason they make more "mistakes" in raising him. They tend to make him do more, and they expect more of him.

This is their first child. And because they are proud parents, they want him to be the best that he can possibly be. They have preconceived ideas of what the perfect child should be, and they want their child to excel. So they push him hard. He must do more chores. He must obey. He must get better grades in school, and he must make his parents proud. If that sounds like an awful lot to expect from a child, well it is. Many times parents expect too much of their first child.

The second child, on the other hand, may even be ignored. By the time the parents have their second child, a lot of the expectations are gone. They relax a little. Their first child seems to be okay. If he is doing all right, then the second child will make it too. The parents aren't as anxious. There is no crisis and no need to worry and fret. He'll be all right. And so it goes for the next child, and the next.

The last child, however, is a different story. By now, the other children are all growing up and, in some cases, have even left the "nest." Then the "baby" comes along, and this child is special to the parents. He/she is their last child, so he/she is loved in a different way.

The parents are older now. They are more settled. They may have "made it" by now. They can take life easy now. They probably have more money at this stage of their lives, and there isn't as much pressure for them to handle. They have learned from their past mistakes (they think), and their last child has a different situation facing him than his older siblings.

So the "baby" is spoiled. He gets coddled. It is not a myth that the older sisters and brothers may be just a little bit jealous. Or they too may baby their little brother or sister as well.

Albert was the oldest child. He had to endure the effects of the abuse more acutely than the others did. He saw bad things happen, and he was old enough to remember them. He had another problem as well because he was a serious child who had inherited the tendency to have schizophrenia.

Even if he had been born to an ideal family, he still would probably have suffered from his illness anyway. In fact, many people develop this illness that have come from ideal families. But Samuel, alas, not only had to suffer from the abuse but from a chemical imbalance in his brain as well. Rheumatic fever could have been the trigger. He had two strikes against him from the beginning.

Even so, today it's possible that a case of schizophrenia like Samuel's could have been treated. Back in the '40s and '50s, many drugs that we take for granted today hadn't been developed yet. Samuel was born too soon.

On the other hand, Jack Junior was lucky. Although he had the same genetic tendency toward mental illness, he did not see too much of the abuse. He also stayed away from the family in his early teens. Therefore, he was able to live a normal life. He married, had children, and became a successful businessman. Even so, he still had problems with his nerves. Throughout his life, he controlled his nervous tendencies by hard physical work and drinking a six-pack of beer every day.

Now, back to Marla. Marla had a disadvantage because she was the youngest child. She also had many fears. How she got those fears is understandable, but she also had no help in dealing with them. If she had seen a competent psychologist at an early age, her whole life could have been turned around. He would have taught her how to control her fears and how they got there in the first place.

As each child develops he/she must learn a certain measure of independence or she will not survive the real world. Marla's fears kept her from doing this. She should have been encouraged to stand on her own. But she wasn't.

As each child grows, providing he/she is in good health, he/she will sooner or later reach out to accomplish something. This is an innate tendency, and most children are born with it. It is only by accomplishing something that the child first gets her taste of the satisfaction of doing something. As she develops, she is feeding her self-esteem.

Marla should have been made to do something, anything: brush her teeth, wash her clothes, anything that would have brought her some measure of self-satisfaction. She missed out on all that.

She missed out on developing her self-esteem. She missed out on experiencing the joy of life, of marriage, of having children, a career. She never experienced the wonder of success, the success of having a happy life.

By coddling Marla, Mom was encouraging her to be lazy, to stay out of school, etc. In short, she was rewarding her for her laziness. She was saying, "Okay, honey, you don't have to go to work, you don't have to go to school. You just sit there. That's all you have to do. I'll take care of everything. Everything will be all right."

So Marla took the easy way (what seemed to be the easy way), but in fact was the way that led to unhappiness and lack of self-worth. Way down in her consciousness, Marla may have known she wasn't doing the right thing. But her mother was letting it happen, and Marla trusted her mother, and it led to nowhere.

Before you judge my mother's actions, however, before blaming her for Marla's illness, let's look at the story from her side. Her only crime was that she loved too much. She had been abused and had no husband to run to for comfort and advice. Marla was in the wrong place at the wrong time. Her mother took away her independence. She had no direction, no counseling. In her ignorance, Mom didn't know what she was doing. She was a victim of circumstances too.

What's more, Marla had an addictive personality. And even the medical profession let her down. When she took the cure for drug addiction at twenty-one, her treatment should've been followed up with counseling. She got none.

The last straw was when a doctor came in the middle of the night to give her a shot to make her sleep. This incompetence was unforgivable, even though she lied to him. It wasn't too late, even at that stage of her life, to turn her life around. Good counseling, even at that time, may have made the difference. But somehow she managed to fall between the cracks.

I had many fears too, but I had the stamina to fight them and win. I had assertiveness. Although I had to live with mental illness, I overcame it each time. I was a fighter.

I learned early in life that accomplishments brought worthwhile rewards. I enjoyed doing well in school and, later on, in my work and marriage. I also sought help from others. Things didn't just come my way. I made good things happen by hard work and patience. Not everything I tried to do was a success. I wasn't able to help my family. Yet I developed enough skills, through the years, to help my children.

CHAPTER 17

My daughter Angel Ann got married to her college sweetheart, and I caught the bouquet.

Then, in 1994, which was a year later, another strong and caring man came into our lives. I met him on a blind date. My friend Anita introduced us. He bought me roses, he bought me chocolates and a teddy bear with a heart attached to it, which said "I love you" on it, and he bought me coffee while I was on the job. He even bought enough coffee for the entire crew. He came over to my house to see me every day.

And when he bought me a diamond ring, I accepted it. Sidney Brown was a widower who understood that I had many problems with my three sick sons, but he married me anyway. We had the sweetest wedding. We got married in a small historical chapel, which was used on special occasions, and rented an antique limousine. We made each other very happy. He came to live with me after the ceremony was over.

By now, Sam had worked in his career for two and a half years. He began to learn how to harness the energy he got from his mania and use it to excel in his career. Then, he gradually moved up the corporate ladder by dedication and hard work.

Sidney knew that, even though Sam had worked in his career for years, he still was afraid of leaving home. Sidney also knew that all he needed was a little push, so he convinced him that it was time he was on his own. The next day, Sam proudly walked out the front door with the classified ads under his arm. Although he was still fearful, he was actually relieved that his past was behind him, and he could move on to his future.

My old car was a wreck, so after the honeymoon, Sidney and I bought a better one. I now had someone to help me, not only financially but with my children as well.

Loius had been on disability for two and a half years and, with medication and behavior modification, was gradually recovering. But he had no car, and it was pitiful to watch this kid, who had worked so hard for a college degree in three majors, applying for various menial jobs on foot. He tried the gas stations, drug stores, department stores, and many others.

While Sidney was purchasing our automobile, he said to me, "Louis will never find a decent job unless he has a proper car." With that, we took Louis to a dealership the next day and informed the proprietor that we wanted a good secondhand car for Louis. Upon hearing this, the dealer brought out a large station wagon that was covered with body rot.

"Louis deserves better than that," Sidney said angrily. So we took Louis to another lot where we chose a beautiful tan Chevrolet Cavalier without a mark on it.

Louis's eyes lit up like the Fourth of July, and he almost cried with gratitude.

"You don't have to pay us back," Sidney said.

A couple of months later, Louis too wanted to leave us. The Jackston Mental Health Center found him a group home to live in. Weeks later, Louis had a steady job as a forklift operator, which he kept for a year and a half until he decided to move in with his brother in Taunton.

He got a job working for Motorola, related to his career field. But he still had a rocky road ahead of him. He still couldn't handle stress, so after having a massive panic attack because he couldn't get along with his brother, he landed back in the hospital for the tenth time. His courage was remarkable. As soon as he left the hospital, he found another job working in the cement industry, and he found himself a place to live.

In the meantime, Jonathan remained at college, living with friends. I only got the chance to see him on the holidays when he seemed to be all right. He had an attack of kidney stones and while he was in Roger Williams Hospital, he told me he had homosexual tendencies and that he had planned on killing himself. After his stay in the hospital, Sidney and I took him to see a psychiatrist who told him he was normal. So back he went to stay with his friends.

Sidney made me see the fact that I could get my medical bills paid for by the Veterans Hospital in Providence, so I started going there for treatment. I found out that I was bipolar too. When I heard that, I burst into laughter. The counselor didn't know what to say about my reaction.

I explained, "I have been struggling with this all my life. In fact, I'm now sixty years old and I found out at last what my problem is. You've finally given it a name. I'm crazy. The whole thing is humorous."

For a while, everything seemed to be fine with my four children, and for three and a half years, Sidney and I were still on our honeymoon. In the meantime, my mother's health started to fail her. I went to visit her on a Tuesday, and upon her insistence, we danced the "Beer Barrel Polka" around her apartment. She seemed fine to me.

On Thursday, I went to visit her again, and I saw my sister-in-law's van parked outside. When I went inside, Barbara, my brother's wife, was preparing to take Mom to the hospital. I told her that I would take her. At the hospital, the doctors tried to operate to remove a "blockage" from her intestines, and they told us there was nothing they could do because the blockage was as hard as cement. The doctor told us she was dying.

Sidney and I went to see her every day. I witnessed to her and told her not to be afraid, that the afterlife was a beautiful place. I told her she would see my brother and grandmother again.

Sidney and I took my sister Marla in to see her one day. She held on to my sister's hand with her right hand, and I held her left hand. Instead of looking at my sister, she was looking at me with pleading eyes. Mom couldn't talk at that time. I finally understood what she wanted me to do.

"Don't worry, Mom, I'll take care of Marla." I didn't want the job, but how could I refuse my mother? Mom slipped into a coma shortly after that, and a week later she was dead. After the funeral, Sidney and I found a nursing home near my house so I could take care of Marla.

I have never regretted my promise to my mother. I see a marked improvement in my sister's condition. I know that Mom went to heaven because, just before she slipped into the coma, she looked up and said, "Ma, Sam." I believe that she actually saw them.

Then, one day Sidney went to Foxwoods Casino, which was only a forty-five-minute drive from our house. He began to go there every day, and his losses were considerable. For years he had kept it a secret from me, but now I saw for the first time that he was a compulsive gambler.

When my checks began to bounce, I didn't know what to do. I shed many tears over this, but I told no one of my plight except his niece Natalie. She kept me from divorcing him because she told me he would only gamble big just before payday because he knew that his checks were about to come in. She loved her uncle and convinced me to give him another chance.

What I did was make it to the bank as soon as the money came in, drew it all out of the bank, and paid all of our bills with money orders. I let the casino checks bounce sky high. Then I placed a stop payment on all the checks that were made out to the casino.

One time, I let them wait for six months for a $200 check, and it was not until they got a collection agency after us that I paid them. Foxwoods got really angry. The next time Sidney went to the casino, they called him into an office. I don't know what was said during that interview, but when Sidney came home that day, he mentioned the fact that he didn't want to go to jail.

It took me three years of constant prayer, but my problem was finally solved! My prayers were answered. From then on I handled the checking account, and he only gambled with the money I gave him and that was always in cash. He never cashed a check at Foxwoods again.

Throughout that period of time, Samuel began to suffer from severe depression. While in depression he used to blame me for his sickness. He called home almost every night. Here is an example of what he was going through: he had thought of killing Christ, impaling him to the cross, and piercing his hands and feet. He did this because he blamed God for his illness.

It was as if Satan himself had entered Sam's mind, trying to take control. Every evil thought imaginable was going over and over in his mind. He was thinking of hacking people with an ax. He wanted to make people bleed and suffer. These evil thoughts kept being implanted in his mind by various means.

He started having thoughts of a conspiracy by the police or his boss at work. He couldn't even watch television because he imagined that everyone on TV was talking about him. They were trying to find a reason to punish him.

He was afraid to talk to children because they might get him in trouble with the police.

The alarming part of the whole thing was the intensity of it. It was relentless and powerful. My heart bled for him, but there was nothing I could do except pray.

One day, Samuel's body became swelled up and turned bright red. He went to Miriam Hospital which specialized in diagnostics. When I went to see him, he looked like he had sunstroke, and when I put my arms around him, he was as hot as a stove.

The doctors informed me that they were very concerned with the "rash," as they called it. Also, his fever had been 105 degrees over a considerable length of time. They got the fever down, and the rash subsided, and the doctors diagnosed it as being Still's disease, which in adults is called rheumatoid arthritis. All this anxiety caused Sam to have a panic attack in the hospital.

After a week, they sent Samuel home. But not for long. Within another week, he had another attack of mania. I called the ambulance to take him to Miriam Hospital again. Sam was talking way out of his mind. He didn't know who he was. I stood out of the cubicle with constant tears on my face because I didn't want him to see me that way. The Miriam Hospital shipped him to the Jane Brown unit of Rhode Island Hospital, where they gave him different medication. Then they sent him home with his family.

Sam was on temporary disability insurance (TDI) at the time, and Sidney and I gave him the chance to stay with us for free. Yet Sam wanted to keep his apartment in Taunton, hoping to return to work soon. After three weeks he returned to his job. The company he worked for gave him the most menial job they could give him because of the numerous times he was calling in sick. He was stacking boxes. This was a very boring job for someone as intelligent as Samuel.

Then the company started to send him on more menial jobs. He was now seriously depressed, but he worked on and off for three years. While Sam was still going through all this, I got an earth-shattering call from Butler Hospital telling me that my son, Jonathan, was there in the intensive care unit. They claimed that he had been stalking a girl named Cathy with the intention of killing her.

The man on the phone told me that Jonathan was schizophrenic. Memories of my brother Sam were flashing through my mind. I was in shock when I called my counselor. She calmed me down and told me that Jonathan was not schizophrenic but was a manic depressive person who was suffering from schizoaffective disorder.

She explained it to me this way: "Picture a horizontal line. One end of the line is normal. Way on the other end, the worst a manic-depressive patient can be is called schizoaffective disorder. Your son is not schizophrenic."

She told me to call back the hospital and ask to speak to his doctor. She also told me that if the doctor is not available, ask to speak to the patient advocate.

I finally got to speak to his doctor, and he confirmed what my counselor had told me. Jonathan was not schizophrenic. After being in the hospital for a week and a half, he came home to live with Sidney and me. He put a restraining order against himself stating that he not go near this girl again. He did this to protect both Cathy and himself.

In the meantime, Sidney's health was failing him. It all started when he went in the hospital for minor surgery to have two benign tumors removed from his neck. During the operation, the doctor cut a nerve by mistake, thereby paralyzing half of his face.

After that, things went from bad to worse. He couldn't eat because he had no feeling on half of his face. Because he didn't eat, he got very weak and started falling down often. I tried everything to get him to eat. I tried to make soft foods, but he only gagged on it. I even got a food grinder, but he wouldn't eat that food because he said it looked like garbage.

I tried so hard to make Sidney eat that I forgot to eat myself. With all this going on in my life, I began to fall apart myself because of a lack of sleep. My doctors had taken me off Depakote because of my terrible tremors. The new medication they gave me couldn't help me to sleep. That, along with constant worry over Jonathan and Sidney, made me end up in a mental ward. I came to the hospital starving and dehydrated.

For the first time in my life, I experienced all the symptoms of my disease to the fullest. I suffered tremendously. I experienced depression and mania and what is called "mixed states," which is a combination of both. Being as it was a veterans' hospital, I was surrounded by men, who made me feel uncomfortable. But before long, I was making them all laugh.

The first thing I did was to make sure that Sidney and Jonathan were cared for. My niece Natalie came over every other day and cooked for Sidney. The VA got a hold of Jonathan's counselors, and they were coming over to the house every day to make sure that he was taking his medication.

It took the doctors three days to find the right medication in order for me to sleep. While I was in the hospital, I wrote the following, trying to explain what it was like to be mentally ill: "I finally am experiencing our disease for the first time. I am fascinated with it. Where the heck am I going? I think at first it was 'worrywart.' I constantly worried about my husband's health until my thoughts simply went around and around all the time, all the time, around and around, all the time. Then strange things began to happen.

"Okay, first it was depression. But what the heck is this? I'll call this phase 'wacko.' I feel giddy all the time, and everything is funny. Then I had what is called 'mixed states.'" It is a combination of laughter and sadness going on in my head. I think I'm experiencing what my boys were suffering from.

I had a beautiful dream last night. Or was it real? It seemed to really have happened. I was lying in bed, as usual, trying to get to sleep.

This is what happened and how I explained it in my notes: "God has allowed me to have a bird's eye view of the whole universe all at once. At the same time I had the knowledge of everything that was happening, the whole works, everything all at once. I knew what everyone was thinking, and I knew what everyone was saying and doing. The catch was, at the same time, I had to feel God's pain."

I even figured out the reason for it all. God is growing us up and is allowing us to have the view. We are his children and he wants us to grow up and be like him someday.

The doctors finally were able to treat me for lack of sleep, and last night I slept the whole night for the first time in months. What a treat! My mind still had to mend though. When I wanted to say something to the guys on the ward, I would begin the sentence, then the thought would leave my head completely, and I couldn't remember what I was going to say. I found this to be very humorous, and I would laugh each time it happened.

CHAPTER 18

The Veterans Hospital dismissed me after an eleven-day stay and sent me home to the many problems I had to face there. I felt up to the challenge.

When I came home from the hospital, I called my brother Jack and demanded a car. He came through for me and brought over my father's ten-year-old Subaru. It was better than nothing. Now, when Sidney went to the casino, I could at least have a vehicle to use.

Jonathan was very ill even though he was a loving person. He did whatever he was told to do. He helped me clean the house, and when warm weather came, he worked in the garden. His counselor advised him to walk, and walk he did. Sometimes he would be gone for eight hours at a time.

Jonathan was so ashamed of his obsessive-compulsive disorder or OCD, that he kept it a secret from me for an entire year. One day, however, he decided to tell me the whole sordid truth.

"Mom," he told me, "When I was a child I got a hold of a pornographic magazine. I studied it. I thought it was okay. I thought that's what people do when they grow up. By the time I realized it was a sin, it was so engrossed in my mind that I could not get those thoughts out of my head. I am now, in my thoughts, a sex pervert. I want to rape every woman, man, child, and even some animals. My mind is a sewer."

I asked him if the medication helped with some of these thoughts, and he told me it did to some extent, but he still had to deal with these thoughts on a daily basis.

I couldn't sleep all that night. I was shocked and in emotional pain.

The next day he told me that he had never acted out these thoughts. He would simply walk away if he felt the temptation or commit himself to Butler Hospital if necessary. That made me feel better.

For two years, Jonathan and I lived together with Sidney. One night there was a loud knock on the door. When I opened the door, there were two policemen who told me that they had a warrant for Jonathan's arrest.

Some guy had exposed himself to two girls at a place called Benny's parking lot. An anonymous call told the cops to check out Jonathan Black. They showed the two girls the photo of Jonathan from his driver's license, and one of the girls identified him from a group of photos.

They carted Jonathan away to jail in handcuffs. Jonathan told me before they did that he didn't commit this crime, and I believed him. He didn't even know where Benny's parking lot in East Greenwich was, and I never let him use the car on Sundays, and the crime was committed on a Sunday. My son was in jail for five days without his medication.

At the court hearing, they released him in my custody. We went through six months of hell until finally, the court decided that Jonathan was guilty after the older of the two girls pointed to him in the courtroom and said that he was the one.

The judge discredited my testimony by saying that I was lying to protect my son. Jonathan got six months' probation, and he was ordered to see a Dr. Pitassi once a week for six months. This was a godsend because Jonathan and I had been looking for a psychologist to help him with his head problems.

Even though Jonathan was not guilty, he now had to try to get a job with a criminal record. I think the whole experience took ten years off my life because I was no longer a happy woman. Jonathan also told me that he was sexually molested five times by other boys in junior high school, and the teachers did nothing.

Also Jonathan and I watched Sidney's health deteriorate. In the first place, he was incontinent. I had to make him wear pads and had to protect our bed by spreading pads on his side of the bed. It didn't do much good because there was a constant smell of urine in our room. I used sprays and even sprinkled perfume on my side of the bed. Sometimes I had to sleep on the couch. But he wanted me to sleep with him. I did so whenever I could.

Then he started choking on his food because of the botched operation that paralyzed half of his face. So I made sure all his food was soft.

The biggest part of his ailment, however, was the fact that he kept on falling down. I got him a cane, and from that a walker, then a wheelchair. This all happened in a matter of months.

Realizing that he needed some form of recreation, I took him to Foxwoods Resort Casino twice a week anyway. But the time came when my only recourse was to take him to a nursing home.

It was a sad day for me, but I found out that, because Sidney was a totally disabled veteran, the charge for the nursing home would be nothing. That meant that I could use his money to pay for the car, and even my sick son. As the weeks went by, I began to feel relieved that Sidney was getting the care that he so desperately needed, and I had more time to spend working around the house. I visited him three times a week, which seemed to satisfy both him and me.

One day Sam called and told me he wanted to move in with us. Things were going bad at work, and he did not like the place he was living in. I welcomed the change of pace. A few days later, he arrived at my doorstep. One day I woke up feeling terrible. I had a cup of coffee and was on my way to getting a second cup when I felt so bad I placed my cup on the counter and passed out.

Jonathan heard the crash as I hit the floor. When he saw me, he called 911. When I came to, I told him to call the rescue.

The ambulance took me to the Veterans Hospital where they found out that my heart was beating erratically. They kept me for five days attached to a heart monitor. Then they tested my heart and found nothing wrong with it. Sam and Jonathan visited me every day and once, when I reached for their hands, my heartbeat returned to normal. The doctors still couldn't figure out what was wrong with me. I passed out five more times when I came home and my children were taking care of me.

Then I caught pneumonia and went back to the hospital for another four-day stay. Sam and Jonathan took me home when I was released, but it took two months for me to be able to work around the house.

My two sons coddled me. They let me sleep on the couch because they didn't want me to fall out of bed. Sam slept on his sleeping bag on the floor. They performed all the necessary household tasks, which included getting me something to eat. I lived mostly on soups.

After the pneumonia, I caught the flu. But by now my body was strong enough to fight back. I got over the flu fairly easily. But it took months for my body to recuperate. I kept getting dizzy spells. Finally the doctor gave me medicine for those spells, but it wasn't until summer came that I felt healthy again.

One day Samuel came home and told us that he had quit his job. He said he couldn't take it anymore.

That was the beginning of a downward spiral for him. Louis was now living in California because he got a job out there. He managed to get Sam a job out there also. Sam drove across the country to take the job. It was very dangerous work, and after almost getting killed, he quit. It lasted only a week.

Before long, Sam and Louis had an argument, and Sam drove back across country again, to home. Now I had to support Sam. It took all of my income just to survive. It was a good thing I had Sidney's disability check. If anything happened to Sidney, I would lose my home.

Another thing that bothered me a great deal was the fact that Louis had turned to devil worship. I know that it was his illness that made him do it in the first place, but the fact that he had joined a coven and was practicing black magic was enough to unnerve me. I had heard enough of devil worship to know that it was almost impossible for one to get out of it, and that was only if he wanted to. Louis was content with his black magic. He didn't believe in heaven or hell. He believed only in the lies that his black magic books told him.

However, since I believe strongly in the power of God, I pray for him daily. Since God does answer my prayers, I have hopes that he will perform some kind of miracle to get Louis back to Christ again because it will take some kind of big miracle to straighten out my son.

My heart ached for him. I keep remembering him as an innocent child. How could this have happened? He was brought up in a Christian household. But the power of Satan is strong. He can lure men into the downward spiral into hell. I won't let this happen to my son. Not if I can help it. My faith in God is strong, and if I have to pray every day for Louis for the rest of my life, I will do so. Sam and Jonathan pray too. Also Sam witnesses to him over the phone every chance he gets.

Sam collected unemployment until the end of August and on September 3, 2004, he filed for social security disability insurance (SSDI). After that, it was an agonizing wait for him to find out if he was eligible. During that time, he applied for and got two more jobs. The first job lasted for two days, and the second lasted only for two hours. Both times he panicked and went into depression. This man could not work for a living due to his mental condition. For the time being at least.

Six months later, his checks started to come in. What a relief for the family budget. Now I could begin to make a double payment on my car, hoping to have it paid for by the time Sidney died. If I could manage to do this I could afford to keep my home until I died. My wish is to die in my own bed with my children, whom I love, around me. And I wanted to go to heaven quickly without placing a heavy burden on my children.

CHAPTER 19

Perhaps the person who came back from the bottom of Satan's pit to make a remarkable recovery is my son Louis. When my husband commissioned him to take care of the whole family, he must have known that Louis was capable of doing it.

But not Louis. He was still in school and had dreams of becoming an astronaut. After graduating, he found he could not get a job. Things went from bad to worse. After Sidney and I bought him a car, he was on his way.

However, he had to start from the bottom. And he certainly reached the bottom. He went into black magic. He joined the Cult of the Psychic Vampire. He believed that he could suck the life out of those around him.

I didn't find out about all this until much later. Louis got a job working for a pipe manufacturing company as a common laborer. This company made pipes big enough for a subway to fit into. For the first two years, he worked in a tunnel, grinding. But then the company discovered how bright he was. He had three degrees: physics, applied math, and chemistry. They made him take a test. He passed the test with a score of ninety-nine. They made him a safety manager. He no longer had to work in the tunnel.

Then one day, Louis called home with the good news that he was a Christian again. Sam, Jonathan, and I had been praying for years for him, but we had never even hoped for such a remarkable answer to our prayers. Louis told me that he was looking for the right church. He decided to join the Roman Catholic Church.

The company then sent him to New York City to build a tunnel under a subway big enough to house a different subway. They sent him and two other men to Germany to check out a machine that would do all the grinding. They came back with news that the machine was a go.

Louis was happy to work in New York because he was now near his family so he could come home for visits often. While in New York, he fell off a catwalk and broke his ankle. He was on crutches for three months. So they gave him a desk job. Even with a cast on his foot, he came home often.

He is a born-again Christian now. He went to church every week without fail, and he frequented all the bookstores he could to build up his library. He worked in New York for one and a half years. Then the company gave him the option of either staying in New York or going to Indianapolis. Louis saw that the job in New York was getting near the end so he chose Indianapolis. He now owned a truck, having lost his car to a New York blizzard while he was trying to make it to church.

He packed up his truck and left piles of boxed books in the basement. On another trip, he came home with another pile of books and enjoyed a two-week vacation with us while we celebrated the holidays. We spent many happy hours together.

He enjoyed working in the middle of the country very much. While there, they sent him to Los Angeles in order to take three tests. These tests, of course, would eventually lead to a promotion.

As a safety engineer, he had to go into the tunnel once in a while. But he was responsible for the safety of the men in the tunnel. Rumors went around about a job in Southern California.

He was in Indianapolis for one and a half years, and they told him he had to go to Los Angeles. He was hardly unpacked. Now he had to pack again. It took a hundred boxes to fit all his books and household paraphernalia in.

These he gave to the movers, and the rest he packed on his truck. The company gave him a month to prepare for the move. Then his friends took him out to a steak dinner. The next day he said goodbye to all his friends.

While Louis was away from home, he called every day. On his trip to California, he called us from every stop. He stayed in hotels three times, and when he reached Los Angeles, he found out that the company had paid for a full month's stay in a hotel, thereby giving him lots of time to look for an apartment.

In Los Angeles, he found many of the gang from New York, which made him feel at home. The job cost $3.5 billion, and it was in its infancy. The drilling had not begun yet. Louis also signed up for Mars 1; he had never had forgotten his childhood dream to go to Mars.

Louis was working in a hard job, but he was thriving on it. He also bought as many translations of the Bible as he could. What's more, he read them all. Louis is flying.

Louis's identical twin brother Samuel is at least as intelligent as he is. However, being mirror twins, they are opposites. Louis is left-handed; Samuel is right-handed. Louis is an introvert; Samuel is an extrovert. Louis is dedicated, and Samuel does not have this gift. However, that does not mean that Samuel is lazy.

Samuel came down with rheumatic fever and was rushed to the hospital. The medicine that the doctors prescribed caused some damage to his pancreas. This was the start of diabetes. With his obsessive-compulsive disorder, he became obsessive about testing his blood sugar at work. When he realized that he couldn't keep a job, he became very depressed.

While in depression, he had severe pains in his chest. He was rushed to Rhode Island Hospital by ambulance. While there, something marvelous happened; he had a near-death experience (NDE). This is how it happened in his own words: "I was laying there attached to a monitor when all of a sudden, I popped out of my body within a tunnel. I could see the doctors working on me, and my body was lying on a cot. Then I popped back into my body only to pop back out of it again. This time I looked down. I could see that I was wearing a white robe that glowed. I couldn't see my feet, only the robe. Then I looked at my arm. It was covered also by the white robe down to my wrist. Then I could see that this silver cord was connected to my navel. Then I popped back into my body again."

The doctors told him that he did not have a heart attack, but his heart's rhythm was interrupted.

Shortly after, they sent him home.

But slowly, gradually through the years, he began to recover from his mental illness. At first he began to buy many books, but he was only reading a few pages in every book. Then he started to go out to buy coffee each morning. Then something marvelous happened: he began to read more and use his computer. He learned how to program.

At this time I had a stroke. After a brief hospital stay, the doctors informed me that they were going to send me to a nursing home for a couple of weeks to recuperate. I agreed.

They sent me to Morgan nursing home. I chose it because it was near to my home. Was I ever wrong! In the three days I was there, I only slept one night. Because I am bipolar, I take pills to get rid of my mania so I could get to sleep at night. They neglected to give me my pills. One day they forgot to feed me. The food was so bad that I couldn't eat it anyway.

I called home and begged Sam to get me out of there. It is a long, involved story but Sam ignored his own health problems and managed to break all the rules in the nursing home and got me out of there. In a pinch, Sam always comes through. Samuel too is learning how to fly.

Angel Ann is my only child that could get married and have children. But she did give me the world's greatest son-in-law, Mark Garrison, and two wonderful grandsons, Aydin and Garrett. They are completely normal. Because of my poor health I can't go and visit them, but Angel sees to it that she visits me every year. I enjoy her visits very much. She and Mark make excellent parents.

She is now living near Louisville, Kentucky, and has recently discovered a Korean church. After taking lessons, she became

Roman Catholic and joined the church. I now have two Roman Catholic children and two Protestant children. I am convinced that they are all going to heaven someday.

Angel is discovering her Korean roots, something that I have always wanted for her. The whole family now belongs to this church, and they pray often.

I am very proud of my daughter. I could not become a missionary, but through the adoption of a foreign child, I feel that I have somehow fulfilled a part of that goal.

Angel suffers from seasonal affective disorder (SAD), but she doesn't let it bother her too much.

Ding ding! The cash register rings, "That will be $211, please." Jonathan proudly shows his food stamps card. By law, he has to keep it for himself. But I always give him $187 a month from my own resources. All this goes to the poor.

Jonathan is doing remarkable for someone with little resources. He collects $677 a month from a disability pension and $187 in food stamps. On top of donating all of the food stamp money, he gives one third of his check to charity. He has to pay me $300 a month for room and board.

He also does all my driving for me since I had five accidents in one year, and I took myself off the road before I would wind up killing someone. On top of this, he does charity work for his church and others.

However, he suffers from depression almost every day. The only reason he cannot work is because of his mental illness. When Louis said that he was the smartest one, he was right.

Perhaps the best way to describe Jonathan is his remarkable personality. He can carry on a conversation with anyone from the governor to a homeless person. He is never at a lack for words. He could talk his way out or into every situation. He has dozens of friends and knows everyone he meets by name.

Everyone at the market we go to knows him. And he loves everyone he meets. He is on the phone for hours chatting with his many friends. Jonathan doesn't have to learn how to fly, he already is flying.

Wow! What a life I had. I wouldn't trade it with anyone. I had two successful marriages with four wonderful children and held some great jobs and I am still alive and healthy at seventy eight. I live in a beautiful home with my two sons, Sam and Jonathan, who live with me and keep me happy and well. I have a maid and a groundskeeper and eat out often at fancy restaurants.

What an adventure my life has been, and I couldn't have done it without God and the right medicine. We pray a lot in my family. God has always been and always will be the most important part of our lives. Mental illness! Pooh! You are only as sick as you think you are. I'm looking forward to heaven with God, angels, and our savior Jesus Christ. Whoever said mental illness is a curse was dead wrong.

My younger brother Jack (I call him Junior) is a multimillionaire. He has a happy marriage with a wonderful wife.

Even Marla has found happiness. We visit her once a week. She is probably the physically healthiest person in the nursing home. She has the run of the place. She eats in the fancy dining hall and takes advantage of all the parties they give. She says her prayers and says she is sorry to God for all her sins. I knows she is heading for heaven. She prays for all of us constantly.

CHAPTER 20

ental illness, I'm sorry to say, is the most feared and the most misunderstood disease in the world. You mention that "so and so"—perhaps a friend or, worse, your child—is neurotic or even psychotic, all sorts of reactions from different people may pop up. His girlfriend may break off with him. Many of his friends will shun him as if he had the plague, or they may act cool toward him. His boss could terminate his employment. (If he has no real reason to do this, he may fabricate one). All this because of fear.

Fear of what? And why? Well, the "why" answer is easy to explain. And it can be stated in one word: media. The only time a mentally ill person makes headlines is, unfortunately, when someone does something horrendous, like rape or murder. But the evidence simply does not bear out the fact that most crimes are committed by people who could not be diagnosed as mentally ill.

Many violent crimes are the result of rage or vengeance, and some criminals act without a conscience because they were taught no morals. Also, social injustice is the cause of many crimes.

The truth is, most mentally ill people are caring, giving, intelligent, and reliable human beings who happen to have a very painful sickness. I know. I have lived with mental illness all around me, all my life. Those dearest to me, including my children and my mother, have or had this disease.

I'm ill myself, although I didn't know I was psychotic until I was sixty. I've been in the service, held responsible jobs (for which I received awards), graduated from college cum laude, and never in my life that I know of, have knowingly or intentionally hurt anyone. In fact, I help anyone I can whom I think needs any sort of help. And so do the mentally ill people I love.

We grieve from tremors, depression, hallucinations, and mania so bad we think of several different things at once. The pain can be much worse than physical pain.

A lot of the pain the mentally ill endure could be ended if people would only understand them and their illness more. This brings us to the "what" side of the question I have posed. What do people fear when they come in contact with a mentally disturbed or emotionally ill person?

They fear the unknown, one of the biggest and greatest fears known to man. They fear because of their ignorance. They don't understand the illness, and worse, they don't want to know more than they have to about this disease because of fear.

People may learn all they can about heart disease prevention or diabetes. People may watch their diets. They may exercise. These things seem "normal." But they fear anything strange or unnatural. Also, the media doesn't help when they call attention to this illness, only when it's related to crime.

If we face the truth about ourselves, we are all a little "strange" in one way or another. Some women (and men) are fanatical housekeepers. Some kids are "lazy" when it comes to schoolwork. Others are overachievers. Some people devote their lives to musical endeavors even though they don't make much money doing it.

Some people very neatly fold their toothpaste tubes, other crush them with a vengeance. Some are neat; others are sloppy. Some can only take orders, while others cannot accomplish anything unless they are allowed to take over the reins. The list goes on and on.

People are as different as the leaves on the trees. Thank God for variety! And each disturbed person is different in his own way. Some are more severely ill than others; some have phobias; others have compulsions. Many live and function well in society hardly knowing they have a problem.

I'm certain that, in time, mentally ill people from all walks of life will be loved and appreciated for the wonderful human beings they are and be given the chance to fit into society without suspicion and discrimination.